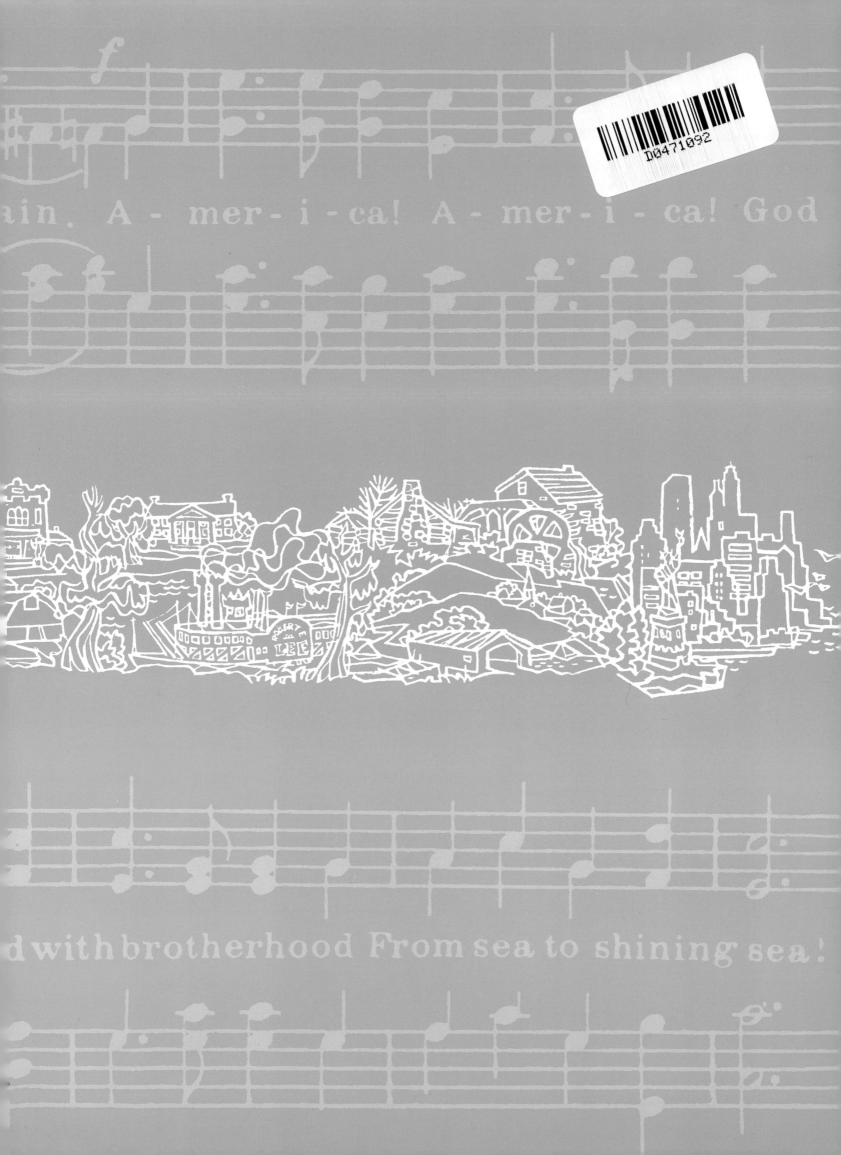

Better Homes and Gardens.

Family Song Book

© Meredith Corporation, 1975. All Rights Reserved.
Printed in the United States of America. First Edition. First Printing.
Library of Congress Catalog Card Number: 74-25580
SBN: 696-00750-9

Note to the reader

This book features a loose-back binding designed especially to make it stay open to the desired page. Should you have any difficulty making the book lie flat while it is on the piano rack, first lay the book on a flat surface. Then, starting at the front and back and moving toward the center, firmly run your finger up and down the book at various intervals—as close as possible to the spine.

Foreword

In my years on the stage, radio, and television, I have probably sung every song in this book. And every time I sing one of these songs, it's a unique experience for me—an opportunity to give my own interpretation to the words and music some gifted American has given to the world.

For as long as I can remember, my greatest desire in life and my most complete happiness has been to sing. I was just four when I first sang with a church choir in my hometown, Washington, D.C. I remember how enthusiastically I sang those songs, even though I was holding the hymnbook upside down. By the time I was eight I was singing for World War I soldiers in the Washington, D.C. area, which may have made me the youngest troop entertainer on record.

My family had hoped that I'd become a nurse, and though I didn't want to disappoint them, I knew my heart belonged to music. So, at seventeen I arrived in New York with no formal musical training, merely the strongest desire anyone ever had to succeed as a singer.

Well, I found out that singers can be good, but the music they sing has to be good, too, or it just doesn't work. That's where American singers are lucky. Over the years, our songwriters have produced some of the most singable, most enjoyable music the world has ever known.

You know, music is very much a part of America, and I guess that's the reason I'm so proud to have been involved in it. I'm proud, too, that I have been able to establish myself as a singer who is also an ambassador of our nation. One of my fondest memories is when President Roosevelt introduced me to the British royal family saying, "This is Kate Smith—this is America."

We have a wonderful country—with great music to represent it. And a lot of that music is here in the pages of this song book. Each one of these songs is an American favorite—not just with singers and musicians, but with everybody. That's why the Better Homes and Gardens *Family Song Book* is bound to be one of the most enjoyable additions you've ever made to your home music library.

Thanks for listenin'.

Kate Smith

Contents

BETTER HOMES AND GARDENS BOOKS

Editorial Director: Don Dooley
Managing Editor: Malcolm E. Robinson   Art Director: John Berg
Asst. Managing Editor: Lawrence D. Clayton   Asst. Art Director: Randall Yontz
Designers: Harijs Priekulis, Faith Berven, Candy Carleton
Text Editors: Jean LemMon (ASCAP), Karen Cure
Picture Researcher: Joan Scafarello
Author: Dick Broderick

Introduction

Man and music are inseparable! For thousands of years music has led armies off to battle, inspired lovers, lulled sleeping babies, and brought smiles to peoples' faces or tears to their eyes. Music has the ability to move people in a way no other art form can. And it isn't relegated to galleries to be enjoyed by a knowledgeable elite, or buried in dusty leather-bound volumes. Music is very much alive. It belongs to everyone and it can be enjoyed by everyone.

As a musical nation, America is still a youngster—but a prodigious one. Only in the last hundred or so years has our country produced music that's definitely American. Prior to that time, the songs were, at best, secondhand versions of what was current in Europe. And, with the notable exception of Stephen Foster, America didn't have any prominent composers or lyricists of her own.

That obviously changed, and as you'll find in this book's section on Great American Composers, we now have an assemblage of songwriters that is comparable to that of any other nation in the world. We have our own composers writing in what has developed into a uniquely American style.

We also have world-famous performing artists, many of whom have groomed a particular song to become their trademark. Songs and entertainers go hand in hand, and in this book you'll find some of the most noteworthy examples of great music and great stars teamed up to make each other a success.

You'll also find a section of typically American sing-along music including several of our country's best-remembered, most-often-sung melodies. The words and melodies of these songs are so familiar that anyone over kindergarten age knows them by heart.

No song book would be complete without including some of America's musical offerings to movies and plays. The American musical has been considered this country's most important contribution to the theater, and you'll understand why when you glance at the list of songs that have moved from Broadway's musicals and Hollywood's movies into the pages of this book.

While Broadway musical scores may be uniquely American, church music is universal. Religion has always played an important part in the music of a country, and our country is no exception. In the section Songs of Religion and Christmas, you'll realize how many famous hymns have been created by American songwriters and just what an impact these writers have had on the music of the church and its celebrations.

But music isn't all serious and scholarly or righteous and religious. Sometimes, music can be just plain fun, and over the years American songwriters have capitalized on the humor or nonsense song. No other country takes its humor as seriously as we do. The result is a section of humorous songs that will keep you chuckling long after you close the song book.

Another area of music that's closely associated with America is our country-and-western songs. They tell of America's grass roots beginnings, of pioneers' courage, and of the struggles and the successes of a people who somehow seem to typify Americans. This song book rounds up some of the best of our country-and-western standards for you to enjoy.

In the same way that music paints pictures of places and people, it also reflects a nation's emotions and attitudes—particularly during times of war. America, just like every great nation of the world, has seen her soldiers march off to battle, usually to a song that expresses the country's patriotism more profoundly than any other medium could. The section on Songs of Battle includes the best of the history-making music that fought beside our soldiers and kept the spirit of America with them.

Section by section, this book represents a musical history of America—her composers, lyricists, performers, and most important her citizens, who have made all these songs popular. This is a song book for all America—for everyone of every age and every degree of musical ability. It's a song book to be enjoyed, not stuck in the piano bench or put on a library shelf. It's music to be played, to be sung, to be loved. It's truly the best of America's great songs.

Great American Composers

American composers may have gotten off to a slow start in their musical endeavors, but they have more than made up for it by creating some of the best music the world has ever known.

For nearly a century, America as a nation was without a composer of the stature of European greats. Remember, however, that the early Americans had things on their minds they considered more important than music. While Beethoven was composing his best-known works in Europe, Americans were staging a tea party in Boston and a battle at Bunker Hill. The music of America at that time was the music of Europe. And for another half-century or so, American music was still a poor extension of European melodies.

Then Stephen Foster came along and earned the title of the "father" of American popular music. Granted, some of Foster's compositions were based on traditional European writing styles, but even these had a flavor that was uniquely American. And other of Foster's works were as American as the stars and stripes.

With Stephen Foster, then, American music had made its debut. But with his death in 1864, our musical progress slowed down temporarily. For the next quarter-century, it was up to the outcasts of society—barroom pianists, strolling guitarists, and minstrels —to sing the blues, preserve the gospels, and hammer out ragtime.

However, it was during this musical slump that some of our greatest creative talents were born, so it was only a matter of time until we had our own world-renowned composers, our own musical style, and our own musical heritage. Between 1885 and 1898, Jerome Kern, Irving Berlin, Cole Porter, and George Gershwin were born, and the future of American music was assured. From this nucleus of creative greats, our country has developed into one of the world's leaders in the field of popular music—with our music being translated into foreign languages and sung the world over.

Ours is still a relatively young nation, and most of its great music is less than a hundred years old. Yet, it's safe to say that people are as familiar with the melodies of Rodgers and Hart, Lerner and Loewe, George M. Cohan, and others as with Beethoven's symphonies. And for a nation that got a late start, that's something.

FOSTER'S MELODIES

Nº 26.

JEANIE WITH THE LIGHT BROWN HAIR

35 Cts NETT

Nº 22. Old Memories 25 cts. nett
Nº 23 Little Ella

Nº 24 Ellen Bayne 35 cts nett
Nº 23 Willie "we have miss'd you".

WRITTEN AND COMPOSED

STEPHEN C. FOSTER.

PITTSBURGH
H. KLEBER & BRO.

CINCINNATI
C. Y. FONDA.

NEW YORK.

PUBLISHED BY FIRTH POND & CO. Nº 547 BROADWAY.

ST. LOUIS
H PILCHER & SONS

Stephen Foster

Jeanie with the Light Brown Hair

With auburn hair and eyes to match, Jane McDowell
never lacked for suitors. Every night, some young man would
shuffle into the McDowell's parlor, grinning and
holding out a bouquet to "Miss Jennie." Sometimes, it was
dreamy-eyed Stephen Foster. At other times, Dick
Cowan, a wealthy lawyer, would sweep in trailing his broadcloth
cape. You'd never have thought that one evening,
when a mix-up brought Foster and Cowan onto the scene at the
same time, Foster would walk out with the lady's
hand, for he didn't look like much and had no prospects to speak
of. But for all that, he was stubborn. On Cowan's
arrival, he plopped into a chair and didn't speak until Cowan left.

The Fosters couldn't live without each other. But they couldn't
live with each other either. The bride was used
to comforts they couldn't afford, even when minstrels everywhere
were singing Stephen's songs. Nor was Jane McDowell
Foster, with her strict Methodist upbringing, that comfortable
with her husband's association with "bawdy"
theatricals. In 1853, after 2½ years together, she packed up and
left. Stephen headed for New York. They were
back together the following year, but not before Stephen had
written and composed "Jennie With The Light Brown
Hair" (the publishers changed it to Jeanie).

After its initial success, "Jeanie's" popularity flickered
until 1941, when a dispute broke out between the
radio networks and ASCAP, the professional society of the
songwriting business. It kept most of the hits off the air,
and "Jeanie," played almost hourly, became a favorite again.

JEANIE WITH THE LIGHT BROWN HAIR

Arranged by Frank Metis

Words and Music by
STEPHEN C. FOSTER

2. I long for Jeanie with the day dawn smile,
   Radiant in gladness, warm with winning guile;
   I hear her melodies, like joys gone by,
   Sighing 'round my heart o'er the fond hopes that die;
   Sighing like the night wind and sobbing like the rain,
   Wailing for the lost one that comes not again:
   Oh! I long for Jeanie and my heart bows low,
   Never more to find her where the bright waters flow.

3. I sigh for Jeanie, but her light form stray'd
   Far from the fond hearts 'round her native glade;
   Her smiles have vanished and her sweet songs flown,
   Flitting like the dreams that have cheered us and gone.
   Now the nodding wild flow'rs may wither on the shore,
   While the gentle fingers will cull them no more;
   Oh! I sigh for Jeanie with the light brown hair,
   Floating, like a vapor, on the soft summer air.

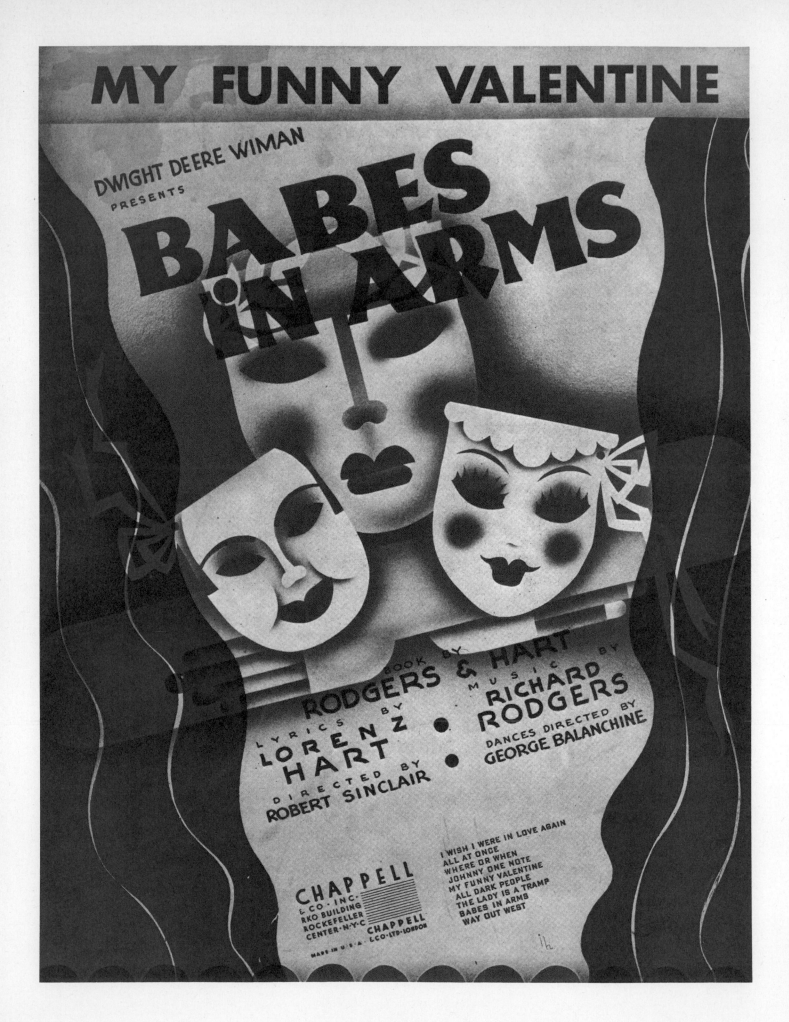

Rodgers and Hart

My Funny Valentine

The careers of many of America's great composers have hinged on the success of one song—that first major breakthrough that established their names and reputations. By the late 1930s, Richard Rodgers and Lorenz Hart were looking for their big hit. Their collaborations had begun making them a living in 1925 when they brought out the irreverent *Garrick Gaieties*, but spectacular success continued to elude them for over ten more years.

In *On Your Toes* (1936), Rodgers and Hart brought celebrated choreographer George Balanchine to Broadway for the first of a series of innovative productions that included *Babes In Arms* (1937). This was the *Garrick Gaieties* all over again, complete with its own brash gang of youngsters. This time, however, they played the offspring of touring vaudevillians who stage an amateur show, and they danced it up in the jazzy Balanchine style. It was in *Babes In Arms* that Mitzi Green, one of the youngsters, introduced "My Funny Valentine," which was innovative at the time because it was written without accompaniment.

Rodgers and Hart did well after that, but by 1943, the partnership had lost its pizzazz. At 48, Hart was depressed and had lost interest in his work. He announced one day that he needed a rest, suggested to Rodgers that he find a new lyrics man, and disappeared. After a frantic search, he was found unconscious in a hotel room, suffering from acute pneumonia. Three days later, he was dead.

Eventually, Rodgers did manage to find a sensational new lyrics man in the person of Oscar Hammerstein II. This tremendously successful partnership resulted in many musical classics including *Oklahoma!* and *Sound Of Music*.

MY FUNNY VALENTINE

Words by
LORENZ HART

Music by
RICHARD RODGERS

Moderately

Verse:

Be - hold the way our fine - feath - ered friend his vir - tue doth pa - rade. Thou

know - est not, my dim - wit - ted friend, The pic - ture thou hast made. Thy

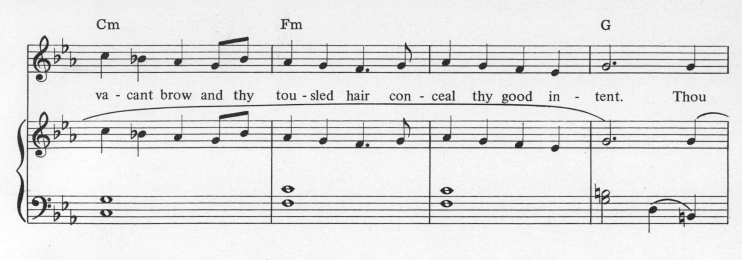

va - cant brow and thy tou - sled hair con - ceal thy good in - tent. Thou

no - ble, up - right, truth - ful, sin - cere and slight - ly dop - ey gent, you're...

Slowly, with expression

Chorus:

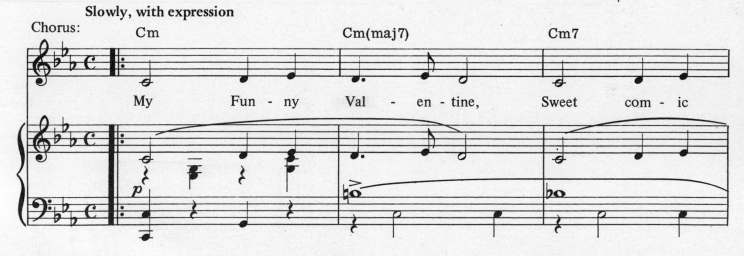

My Fun - ny Val - en - tine, Sweet com - ic

Val - en - tine, You make me smile with my

ON THE STREET WHERE YOU LIVE

Music by FREDERICK LOEWE   Lyrics by ALAN JAY LERNER

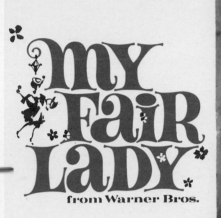

my Fair Lady
from Warner Bros.

Key of B♭

Also Published Separately

From the Warner Bros. Picture
SHOW ME
ON THE STREET WHERE YOU LIVE
I COULD HAVE DANCED ALL NIGHT
WITH A LITTLE BIT OF LUCK
WOULD'NT IT BE LOVERLY
THE RAIN IN SPAIN
GET ME TO THE CHURCH ON TIME
I'VE GROWN ACCUSTOMED TO HER FACE

435000-101

PRICE
95¢

STARRING AUDREY HEPBURN REX HARRISON
CO STARRING STANLEY HOLLOWAY WILFRID HYDE-WHITE GLADYS COOPER JEREMY BRETT
AND THEODORE BIKEL FROM THE BERNARD SHAW PRODUCTION & CECIL BEATON CHOREOGRAPHY BY HERMES PAN MUSIC SUPERVISED BY ANDRE PREVIN
PLAY BY COSTUMES BY
MUSIC BY BOOK, LYRICS & SCREENPLAY BY PRODUCED BY
FREDERICK LOEWE ALAN JAY LERNER JACK L WARNER
DIRECTED BY GEORGE CUKOR TECHNICOLOR® SUPER PANAVISION® 70

CHAPPELL & CO., INC.
609 FIFTH AVENUE, NEW YORK 17, N. Y.

On the Street Where You Live

For years, the songs of Alan Jay Lerner and Frederick Loewe have been performed and recorded the world over. Their hit shows include some of the greatest that Broadway and Hollywood have ever produced, including *Brigadoon, Paint Your Wagon, Camelot*, and of course, *My Fair Lady*.

Their 1956 hit, *My Fair Lady*, gave the songwriting team more challenges than most artists would be willing to tackle. First, there was the Shaw play *Pygmalion*, which was a difficult vehicle. (Cole Porter and Richard Rodgers predicted that a musical version would be a colossal bore.) A second challenge was the characters of stern, woman-hating Professor Higgins and the brash flower girl, Eliza Doolittle—neither of whom were typical Broadway musical personalities. And finally, there was the difficulty in setting the play. One of these set problems was turned into an asset with the song "On The Street Where You Live."

There are times during the course of a performance when scenery has to be changed, not between acts, but during acts. Such was the case in *My Fair Lady* when, while the grips moved scenery behind a closed curtain, the juvenile lead, Michael King, sang his song of adoration for the flower girl turned deb. With a song such as "On The Street Where You Live," the stage wait wasn't even noticed. As a matter of fact, it became one of the highlights of the show, which only proves that genius does have the ability to make silk purses out of sow's ears.

My Fair Lady was the culmination of Lerner and Loewe's 15-year development, and its refinement and sophistication reveal some of the objectives toward which the two songwriters were working all that time.

ON THE STREET WHERE YOU LIVE

Words by
ALAN JAY LERNER

Music by
FREDERICK LOEWE

Refrain: *(slowly)*

the tow - er - ing feel - ing, ___ Just to know ___ some-how you are

near! ___ The o - ver-pow-er-ing

feel - ing ___ That an - y sec-ond you may sud-den-ly ap -

pear! ___ Peo - ple stop and stare, ___ they don't

Had Hoagy Carmichael been able to concentrate on his studies, "Star Dust," the most recorded song in the history of American music, might not exist today. While at the Indiana University law school in Bloomington, he had tried to persuade himself that music was kid stuff and had even turned down a music publisher's job offer. He did sell the publisher one of his creations, though, and pretty soon he was hearing it everywhere. The more he heard it, the better it sounded. In no time, he was back in Bloomington writing new tunes and, at the same time, getting to know one Dorothy Kelly. But because Hoagy couldn't promise her the security she wanted, they parted. Many an evening in 1927, Hoagy would sit alone on the I. U. "spooning wall" and think about things. Then one night, "Star Dust" drifted into his head.

It didn't become popular until 1929, when the Mitchell Parrish lyrics were added. And with the 1935 Artie Shaw recording, it embarked on a career that saw it recorded over 500 times in more than 50 arrangements with lyrics in 40 languages. As Carmichael recalls, "This melody was bigger than I. It didn't seem a part of me. Maybe I hadn't written it at all. To lay my claims, I wanted to shout back—maybe I didn't write you, but I found you."

STAR DUST
ETOILE D'AMOUR

Words by
MITCHELL PARISH
French translation by
Yvette Baruch

Music by
HOAGY CARMICHAEL

Slowly, with expression

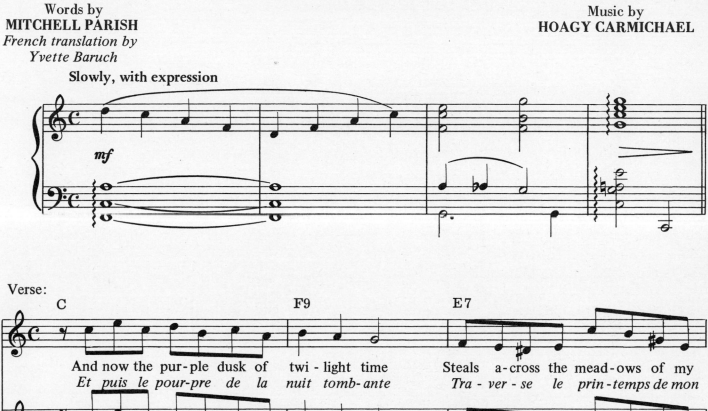

Verse:

And now the pur-ple dusk of twi-light time Steals a-cross the mead-ows of my
Et puis le pour-pre de la nuit tomb-ante Tra-ver-se le prin-temps de mon

heart, High up in the sky the lit-tle stars climb,
coeur, Les é-toiles com-men-çent à grimp-er au ciel,

Chorus:

Some-times I won-der why I spend the lone-ly night
Sou - vent le si - lence de la nuit ré - pète ton nom

dream-ing of a song? The mel - o - dy haunts my rev - er - ie,
comme un - e chan-son, Sa mel - o - die hante ma rêv - er - ie,

And I am once a - gain with you,_____ When our love was new,
Mon rêve me trans-porte dans tes bras,_____ Quand l'a - mour fût jeune,

and each kiss an in - spi - ra - - tion, _____ But
et chaque bai - ser in - spi - ra - - tion, _____ *Les*

that was long a - go, now my con - so - la - tion is in the Star. Dust of a
ann - ées sont pa - ssées et ma con - so - la - tion s'é - leve à l'é - toile d'une chan-

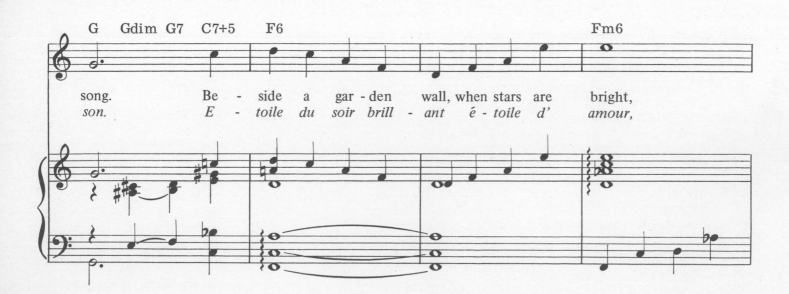

song. Be - side a gar - den wall, when stars are bright,
son. E - toile du soir brill - ant é - toile d' *amour,*

A FOGGY DAY

George Gershwin

A Foggy Day

Any list of great American composers would have to include George Gershwin. Here was a musical genius who in his scant 18 years of music writing composed hits for vaudeville, Broadway musicals, and movies as well as serious music for piano and orchestra. No other American composer was so varied in his musical accomplishments.

It has been said of Gershwin that "of all our composers in the larger forms, he was the most American in feeling and expression, utilizing the native idioms of jazz and blues, adapting the rhythmic effects of snycopation and the melodic rightness of the true folk song." Gershwin earned the highest respect from fellow composers as well as from an adoring public who applauded all his music, from his first hit, "Swanee" to one of his last, "A Foggy Day."

"A Foggy Day," like so many other of Gershwin's songs, was a collaboration with his brother Ira—this particular one was released in the 1937 movie *A Damsel In Distress.* He never fully realized what an impact the song would have on millions of appreciative listeners, though, because he died of a brain tumor six months before its debut.

Though Gershwin was aware of the popularity of his music, he harbored a rather skeptical attitude toward its survival. The writer, in 1932, said, "Unfortunately, most songs die at an early age and are soon completely forgotten by the selfsame public that once sang them with such gusto. The reason for this is they are sung and played too much when they are alive, and cannot stand the strain of their very popularity." Many of Gershwin's songs have proved their composer wrong. They live on and on.

A FOGGY DAY

Words by
IRA GERSHWIN

Music by
GEORGE GERSHWIN

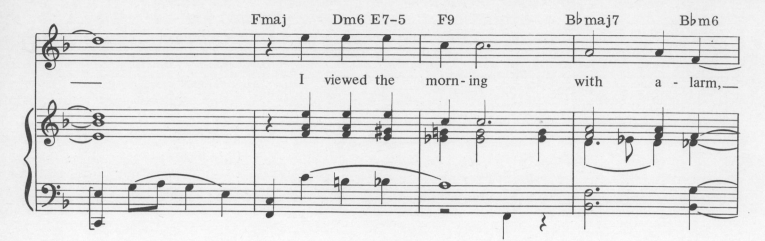

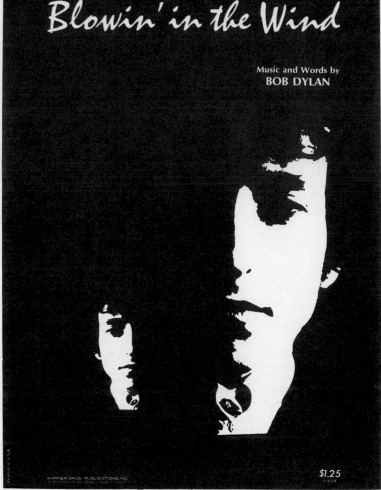

Bob Dylan

One of the best of the protest songs of the sixties, "Blowin' In The Wind" is songwriter Bob Dylan's reaction to the tensions and conflicts of American society at the time. But the title could have just as easily described his own life up to that point.

Born in 1941, Bob Dylan started running away from home when he was 10. By 13, he was working with a carnival. He got to California by hitching and riding the rails, and it was there that he heard Woody Guthrie perform his gutsy protest songs. The experience impressed Dylan so much that the last time he left home it was to visit the dying Guthrie in New York.

For the next couple of years, Dylan blew around New York, sleeping in subways or staying with friends, wearing old clothes because he couldn't afford anything better, and never eating too much. When he could, he would perform in coffeehouses, but he never got paid very well and made no waves—there were dozens of other minstrels around Greenwich Village at that time.

Unlike most of them, Dylan got a lucky break—one that took him all the way to the top—when a critic discovered him in 1961. This discovery led to a record contract and concert bookings.

Fame found Dylan in 1963 after Peter, Paul, and Mary's recording of "Blowin' In The Wind" had sold nearly two million records and won two Grammy awards.

BLOWIN' IN THE WIND

Words and Music by
BOB DYLAN

Bright, spirited

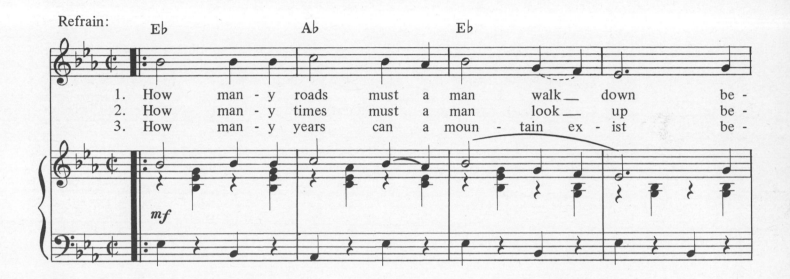

Refrain:

1. How man-y roads must a man walk down be-
2. How man-y times must a man look up be-
3. How man-y years can a moun-tain ex-ist be-

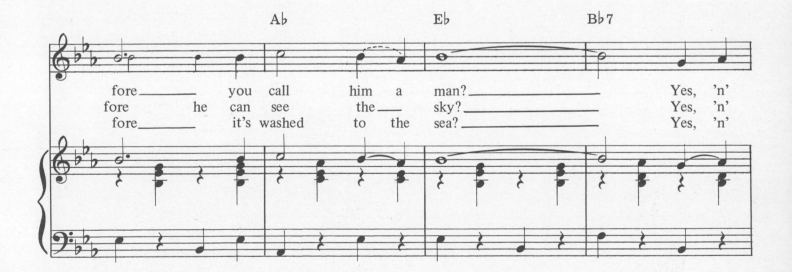

fore you call him a man? Yes, 'n'
fore he can see the sky? Yes, 'n'
fore it's washed to the sea? Yes, 'n'

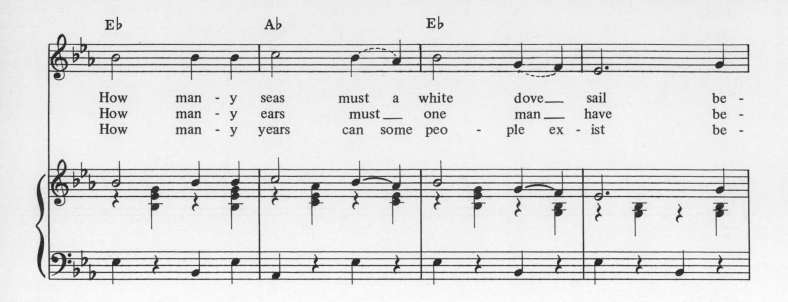

Eb   Ab   Eb

How man - y seas must a white dove__ sail be -
How man - y ears must__ one man__ have be -
How man - y years can some peo - ple ex - ist be -

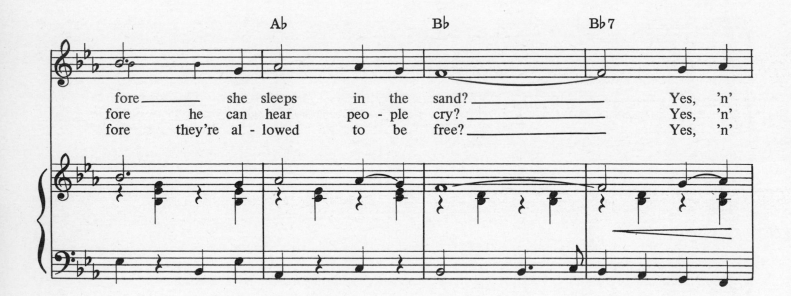

Ab   Bb   Bb 7

fore____ she sleeps in the sand? _____ Yes, 'n'
fore he can hear peo - ple cry? _____ Yes, 'n'
fore they're al - lowed to be free? _____ Yes, 'n'

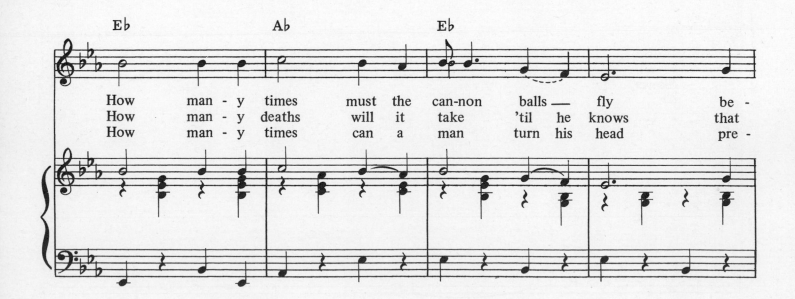

Eb   Ab   Eb

How man - y times must the can-non balls __ fly be -
How man - y deaths will it take 'til he knows that
How man - y times can a man turn his head pre -

More Songs by Our Great Composers

THE BEST THINGS IN LIFE ARE FREE

Verse
There are so many kinds of riches,
And only one of them is gold,
The wealth you miss, remember this,
Worthwhile things cannot be bought or sold.

Chorus
The moon belongs to ev'ry one,
The Best Things In Life Are Free,
The stars belong to ev'ry one
They gleam there for you and me.
The flowers in spring,
The robins that sing,
The sunbeams that shine,
They're yours, they're mine!
And love can come to ev'ry one,
The Best Things In Life Are Free.

Words and Music by B. G. DeSylva, Lew Brown, and Ray Henderson

Copyright 1927 by DeSylva, Brown & Henderson. Copyright renewed, assigned to Chappell & Co., Inc.

Published in the United States by joint agreement with Chappell & Co., Inc. and Anne-Rachel Music Corporation.

POOR LITTLE RHODE ISLAND

Poor Little Rhode Island,
You're the largest one by far,
The other forty nine, they glimmer and they shine,
But you're my favorite star.
Although you're teentsy weentsy
Poor Little Rhode Island,
Let all the Texans 'yipiay,'
You're still the best part of this land I dearly love,
And I'll include Ioway.
They've written songs about the South,
They've written songs about the North,
And I have heard them say there's nothing finer
Than Carolina in the morning,
But how about the nights in
Poor Little Rhode Island,
Be careful if you're fancy free,
In Providence one day, she stole my heart away.
I dream of her constantly
Let the sun shine bright on your Old Kentucky Home,
Rhode Island's the place for me!

Words by Sammy Cahn   Music by Jule Styne

© Copyright 1944 & 1962 by Skidmore Music Co., Inc. Copyright renewed.

TEA FOR TWO

Verse
I'm discontented with homes that are rented,
So I have invented my own;
Darling, this place is a lover's oasis,
Where life's weary chase is unknown.
Far from the cry of the city,
Where flowers pretty caress the streams,
Cosy to hide in, to live side by side in.
Don't let it abide in my dreams.

Chorus
Picture you upon my knee,
Just Tea For Two, and two for tea,
Just me for you, and you for me alone.
Nobody near us to see us or hear us,
No friends or relations on weekend vacations,
We won't have it known, dear,
That we own a telephone, dear.
Day will break and you'll awake,
And start to bake a sugar cake,
For me to take for all the boys to see.
We will raise a family,
A boy for you, a girl for me,
Oh, can't you see how happy we would be?

Words by Irving Caesar   Music by Vincent Youmans

© Copyright 1924 by Harms, Inc. Copyright renewed.

I LOVE PARIS

Verse
Ev'ry time I look down this timeless town,
Whether blue or grey be her skies,
Whether loud be her cheers, or whether soft be her tears,
More and more do I realize:

Chorus
I Love Paris in the springtime, I Love Paris in the fall,
I Love Paris in the winter, when it drizzles,
I Love Paris in the summer, when it sizzles,
I Love Paris ev'ry moment, ev'ry moment of the year,
I Love Paris, why, oh why do I love Paris?
Because my love is near.

Words and Music by Cole Porter

Copyright © 1953 by Cole Porter. Sole Selling Agent: Chappell & Co., Inc.

LULLABY OF BROADWAY

Chorus 1
Come on along and listen to
The Lullaby Of Broadway.
The hip hooray and ballyhoo,
The Lullaby Of Broadway.
The rumble of a subway train,
The rattle of the taxis,
The daffydils who entertain
At Angelo's and Maxie's.
When a Broadway baby says "Goodnight,"
It's early in the morning,
Manhattan babies don't sleep tight
Until the dawn:
Goodnight, baby, goodnight, milkman's on his way.
Sleep tight, baby, sleep tight, let's call it a day. Hey!

Chorus 2
Come on along and listen to
The Lullaby Of Broadway.
The hi-dee-hi and boop-a-doo,
The Lullaby Of Broadway.
The band begins to go to town,
And ev'ryone goes crazy,
You rock-a-bye your baby 'round
'Til ev'rything gets hazy.
"Hush-a-bye, I'll buy you this and that,"
You hear a daddy saying,
And baby goes home to her flat
To sleep all day:
Goodnight, baby, goodnight, milkman's on his way.
Sleep tight, baby, sleep tight, let's call it a day,
Listen to the lullaby of old Broadway.

Words by Al Dubin   Music by Harry Warren
© Copyright 1935 by M. Witmark & Sons. Copyright renewed 1950.

LET'S FALL IN LOVE

Verse
I have a feeling, it's a feeling I'm concealing, I don't know why;
It's just a mental, incidental, sentimental alibi.
But I adore you, so strong for you,
Why go on stalling? I am falling, love is calling, why be shy?

Chorus
Let's Fall in Love, why shouldn't we fall in love?
Our hearts are made of it, let's take a chance, why be afraid of it?
Let's close our eyes, and make our own paradise.
Little we know of it, still we can try to make a go of it.
We might have been meant for each other,
To be or not to be, let our hearts discover,
Let's Fall In Love, why shouldn't we fall in love?
Now is the time for it while we are young, Let's Fall In Love.

Words by Ted Koehler   Music by Harold Arlen
© Copyright 1933 by Bourne Co., New York, N.Y. Copyright renewed.

JUST ONE OF THOSE THINGS

Verse
As Dorothy Parker once said to her boyfriend,
"Fare thee well!"
As Columbus announced when he knew he was bounced,
"It was swell, Isabelle, swell!"
As Abelard said to Eloise,
"Don't forget to drop a line to me, please!"
As Juliet cries in her Romeo's ear,
"Romeo, why not face the fact, my dear!"

Chorus
It was Just One Of Those Things,
Just one of those crazy flings.
One of those bells that now and then rings,
Just One Of Those Things.
It was just one of those nights,
Just one of those fabulous flights,
A trip to the moon on gossamer wings,
Just One Of Those Things.
If we'd thought a bit of the end of it
When we started painting the town,
We'd have been aware that our love affair
Was too hot not to cool down.
So goodbye, dear, and Amen,
Here's hoping we meet now and then,
It was great fun,
But it was Just One Of Those Things.

Words and Music by Cole Porter
© Copyright 1935 by Harms Inc. Copyright renewed.

SWANEE

I've been away from you a long time,
I never thought I'd miss you so.
Somehow I feel your love was real,
Near you I long to be.
The birds are singing, it is song time,
The banjos strummin' soft and low.
I know that you yearn for me too;
Swanee, you're calling me.

Chorus
Swanee! How I love you, how I love you,
My dear old Swanee.
I'd give the world to be
Among the folks in D-I-X-I-E-ven now my
Mammy's waiting for me, praying for me,
Down by the Swanee.
The folks up north will see me no more
When I go to the Swanee shore.

Trio
Swanee! Swanee!
I am coming back to Swanee.
Mammy! Mammy!
I love the old folks at home.

Words by Irving Caesar   Music by George Gershwin
© Copyright 1919 by New World Music Corp. Copyright renewed.

Songs Identified with Entertainers

Nothing brings back memories more quickly than music. Songs are associated with certain places, special people, and times and situations that are happy and sad. All it takes is a few bars of a familiar song to re-create near-forgotten occasions or sensations.

It's no wonder then that in the early days of vaudeville, performers worked so hard to come up with one song that could become their trademark—something that would bring them to the people's minds and keep them there. It may have been the first bit of subtle advertising, but it worked. And without this association, the world might have lost some great standards and some great stars.

Who can hear "Inka Dinka Doo" and not think of Jimmy Durante, or "Me And My Shadow" without seeing the crumpled hat and shuffle that signaled Ted Lewis on stage? And no matter who performs "Love In Bloom," or how it's performed, the image always will be that of Jack Benny and his violin. The theme song always has been an integral part of show business.

Without realizing it, this same musical identification is going on today in another area—television. Catch a line of a snappy, often-repeated commercial jingle and you know instantly what product is being advertised. Or hear the opening theme from one of today's popular programs and without seeing the screen you know what's about to start. It's all based on music and people's association with it. And it is for this reason that thousands of American songwriters work to develop a few bars of music that will stick with their audience and sell everything from soap to soap operas. It's no longer artist and song, but product or program and song.

When Crosby crooned "Where The Blue Of The Night Meets The Gold Of The Day" or when Cagney strutted his way through "You're A Grand Old Flag," musical history was made. Hearts warmed everytime Judy Garland sang "For Me And My Gal," and those same hearts were tugged by Al Jolson's "Anniversary Song." These are the singers and these are their songs, and to say which made the other a hit is nearly as complex as the question, "Which came first, the chicken or the egg?" Maybe it doesn't matter. Maybe the important thing is that the singer and song found each other.

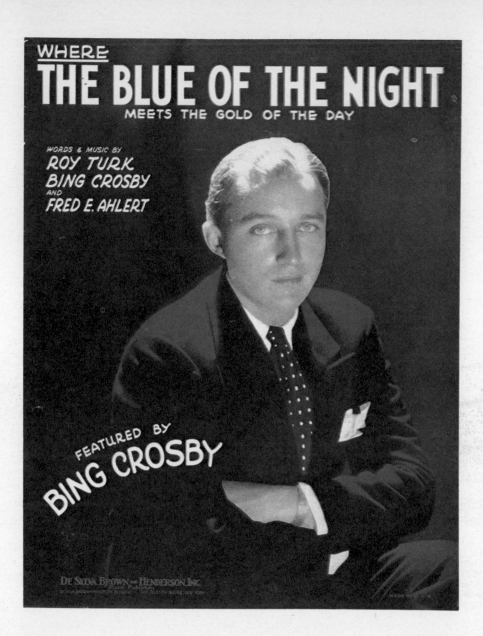

Every era has its superstar. In the twenties it was Russ Columbo, in the sixties the Beatles, and in between, the music throne has been held periodically by stars such as Frank Sinatra, Elvis Presley, and Bing Crosby.

The mere mention of Bing Crosby's name is enough to bring to mind the soft, caressing strains of "Where The Blue Of The Night Meets The Gold Of The Day." It not only was Crosby's theme song, it was co-authored by the singer himself. In 1931 he teamed up with Roy Turk and Fred Ahlert to produce the song that showcased his "ba ba buh" scat vocals—a trademark that he developed during his days as a vocalist with Paul Whiteman.

Those early days, first as a member of The Rhythm Boys and later as a soloist, had a very strong influence on what we know as the Crosby style. Jazz, with its syncopation, was picking up momentum, and it was the perfect augmentation for the cool smoothness of a ballad singer. When the velvety Crosby sound was rendered with a jazz-flavored lilt, it became a winning combination.

Today, it's hard to imagine that Harry Lillis Crosby wasn't always a superstar, but when he made his first appearances, Bing was put down as just another undistinguished singer, much as some rock singers of today are looked down at by the older generation. However, with his stardom won, Crosby has gone on to become an American legend, as has his theme song.

WHERE THE BLUE OF THE NIGHT

MEETS THE GOLD OF THE DAY

Words and Music by
ROY TURK, BING CROSBY
and **FRED E. AHLERT**

Moderately

Verse:

Why must I live in dreams _____ of the days that I
Mem-'ries come back to me _____ of a sun-set be-

used to know? _____ Why can't I find
hind a hill. _____ Each new born day

If on-ly I could see her, _____ Oh, how

hap-py I would be! _____ Where The Blue Of The

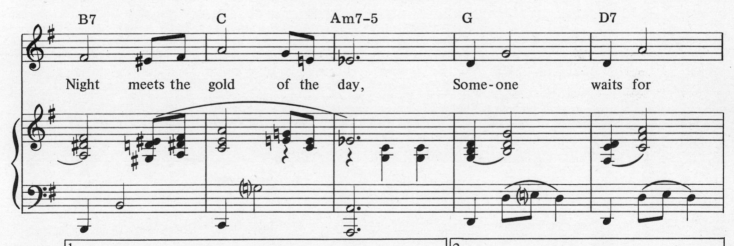

Night meets the gold of the day, Some-one waits for

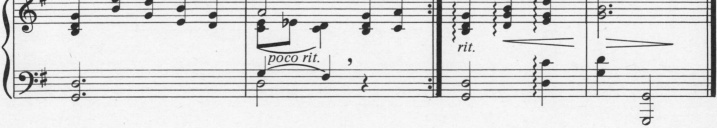

me. _____ Where The   me. _____

Ted Lewis

Me and My Shadow

It's no easier to separate Ted Lewis from "Me And My Shadow" than it would be to separate you and your shadow. No matter how this song is performed or by whom, the image that comes to mind is the quiet entertainer with the battered top hat and opening question, "Is everybody happy?"

In a way, it's remarkable that someone who wasn't really a singer at all should make such a lasting impression as the performer of a particular song. Lewis was primarily a band leader—a good one—in an era loaded with bands and most of them good. But today, Lewis is remembered as an entertainer rather than baton man to a group of musicians.

Lewis never really professed to be a singer—he talked his repertoire in a smooth, blissful manner with his beat-up hat and gliding soft shoe. But when he ambled out on stage and the band started the intro to "Me And My Shadow," this non-singer held every audience captive. In fact, with the personality and artistry of Ted Lewis, the song took on a meaning even its writers, Billy Rose, Al Jolson, and Dave Dreyer, hadn't been aware of.

Over the years, a lot of singers, most more accomplished than Lewis himself, have mimicked Ted Lewis doing "Me And My Shadow." But no one has ever attempted to do the song except as Lewis captured it. His identification with the song is probably the closest meld of music and artist that has ever been achieved by anyone.

Ted Lewis was known in show biz' as "The High Hat Tragedian of Song," but that was only a title for the theater marquee. The truth of Ted Lewis's career is not one of tragedy, but of happiness—for himself and millions of fans. When he asked, "Is everybody happy?", the answer was always "Yes"!

ME AND MY SHADOW

Words by
BILLY ROSE

Music by
AL JOLSON and
DAVE DREYER

George M. Cohan had long since bowed to the wishes of outraged patriotic societies and changed his "You're A Grand Old Rag" to the title we know today by the time James Cagney made the song his personal property in the 1942 film *Yankee Doodle Dandy*. Now, it's hard to think of anything about Cohan without remembering Cagney talking it up out of the corner of his mouth, prancing down stage, and twirling a bamboo cane. Cagney caught the energy of the man who used to bark at his dancers "Speed! Let's have speed!" and — more important — Cohan's very real patriotism. The portrayal brought back old times for the thousands who had seen the legendary performer on stage — and snatched a well-deserved Oscar in the process.

For Cohan, the movie's flattering version of his life was a surprise. And Cagney's portrayal of his younger self moved him so much that a few months after Cohan first saw the film, he went back to Broadway. While his nurse waited in a taxi, he ducked into a movie house where Cagney was delivering the famous Cohan line: "My mother thanks you, my father thanks you, my sister thanks you, and *I* thank you." That was the last time Cohan gave his regards to Broadway. He died a few months later, in November, 1942.

YOU'RE A GRAND OLD FLAG

Words and Music by
GEORGE M. COHAN

There's a feel-ing comes a-steal-ing, and it sets my brain a-reel-ing, When I'm
I'm a crank-y hank-y pank-y, I'm a dead square, hon-est Yan-kee, And I'm

list'-ning to the mu-sic of a mil-i-ta-ry band; An-y
might-y proud of that old flag that flies for Un-cle Sam; Though I

Revisions by Mary Cohan.

rah!   Hur - rah!   We'll   join   the   ju - bi - lee,   And
rah!   Hur - rah!   For   ev - 'ry Yan - kee   Tar   And

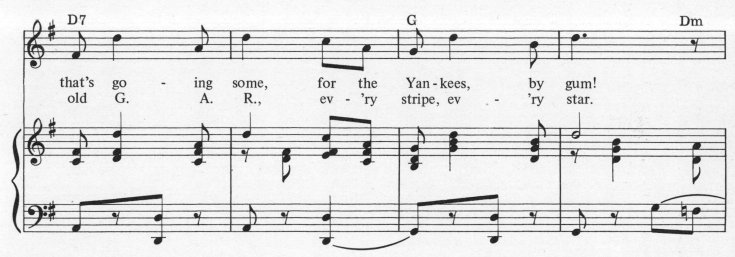

that's   go -   ing   some,   for   the   Yan - kees,   by   gum!
old   G.   A.   R.,   ev - 'ry   stripe, ev -   'ry   star.

Red,   White   and   Blue,   I   am   for   you;
Red,   White   and   Blue,   Hats   off   to   you;

Hon - est, You're   A   Grand   Old   Flag! _____
Hon - est, You're   A   Grand   Old   Flag! _____

Chorus:

You're A Grand Old Flag, you're a high fly - ing flag; And for-
ev - er, in peace, may you wave;_____ You're the
em - blem of the land I love, The
home of the free and the brave._____ Ev - 'ry heart beats

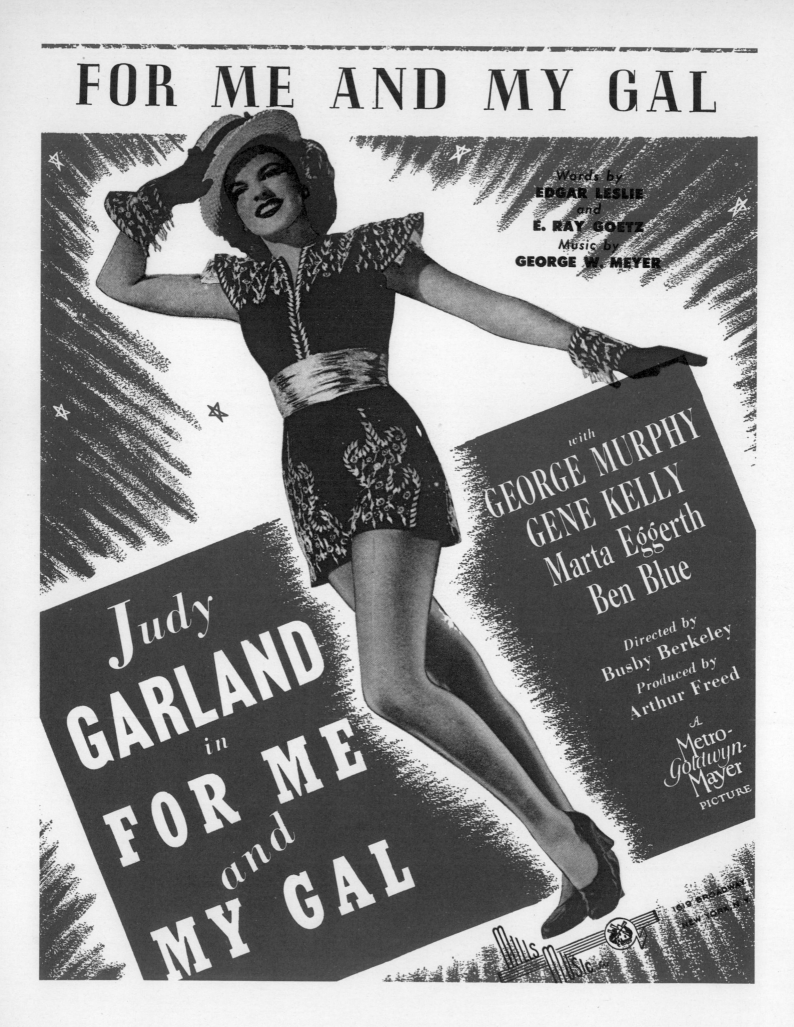

Judy Garland

For Me and My Gal

Written in 1917 by George Meyer, "For Me And My Gal" had
already sold nearly three million copies of sheet music
and had been sung by such famous names as Al Jolson, Eddie
Cantor, George Jessel, and Belle Baker by 1942.
But when Judy Garland, fresh from a triumph as Dorothy in *The
Wizard Of Oz*, took it in hand, millions of people
forgot they'd ever heard it before. You wouldn't have expected
that from such a youngster—but then Judy was a
veteran, having started her stage career at the age of three.

That Judy had a special sort of talent was pretty
much unquestioned. But early in her career, no one appreciated
her ability to reach and charm an audience. In her
teens, she spent her time at MGM churning out low-budget
school days romances with Mickey Rooney. She might
have passed out of fashion along the way had not MGM been
desperate to find its own Shirley Temple. Just as
various studios dug up blondes in the days of Marilyn Monroe,
MGM dolled Judy Garland up in flounces and ruffles
and called her their little sweetheart. That was in *Broadway
Melody Of 1938*, and in her happy-birthday song to Clark
Gable, "You Made Me Love You," she almost stole the show from
Sophie Tucker, Eleanor Powell, and Robert Taylor.

When it came time to cast *Wizard Of Oz*, however, MGM went
after Twentieth Century Fox's Shirley Temple.
This deal eventually collapsed, though, so Judy played Dorothy.
The Oscar that she won for the part sent her on to many
bigger and better things, among them *For Me And My Gal*,
in which she got her first star billing. For George
Meyer, the title song was an end of sorts—it was his wife's
epitaph. But for Judy, it was a big beginning.

FOR ME AND MY GAL

Words by
EDGAR LESLIE and
E. RAY GOETZ

Music by
GEO. W. MEYER

Moderately

Verse:

What a beau-ti-ful day_____ for a wed-ding in May!_____
See the rel-a-tives there_____ look-ing o-ver the pair!_____

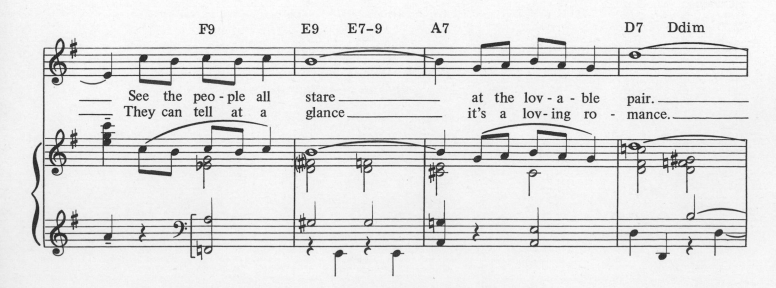

___ See the peo-ple all stare_____ at the lov-a-ble pair._____
___ They can tell at a glance_____ it's a lov-ing ro-mance._____

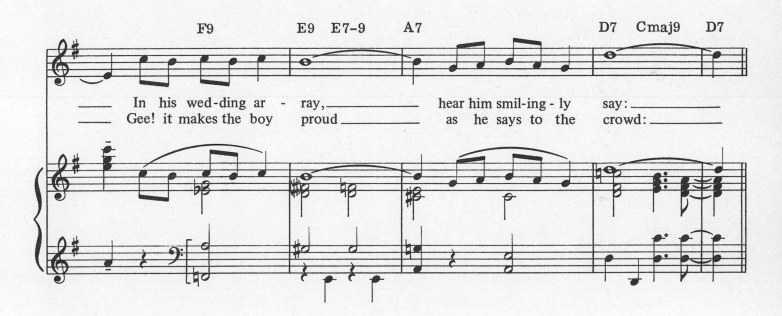

The birds are sing - ing ____ For Me And My Gal. ____

Ev -'ry-bod-y's been know - ing, ____ To a wed - ding they're go - ing,

And for weeks they've been sew - ing, ____ Ev -'ry Su - sie and Sal. ____

They're con - gre - gat - ing ____ For Me And My Gal, ____

The Par - son's wait - ing _____ For Me And My Gal. _____

_____ And some - time I'm goin' to build a lit - tle home for two, _____ For

three or four _____ or more, In love - land _____ For Me And My

Gal. The bells are Gal. _____

Al Jolson, like so many other entertainers, reached the pinnacle of stardom, then slumped into obscurity. It was his hit "Anniversary Song" that put him back in the spotlight.

As a blackface singer and comedian, Jolson had no peer, and his career was studded with one accomplishment after another. It was Jolson who rescued George Gershwin and Irving Caesar's "Swanee" and made it a tremendous hit.

Two years later, Jolson again became a hit-maker with the song "My Mammy." According to a reviewer, "When he sank down on one knee and beseeched his mammy to forgive him, the whole nation jumped to its feet to applaud."

Jolson's next hit was a song he wrote with Bud De Sylva, Lew Brown, and Ray Henderson. The song was "Sonny Boy," a last-minute replacement for a loser in the sound track of *The Singing Fool*. And, of course, Jolson made history with his starring role in the first talking movie, *The Jazz Singer*. But after his great successes of the twenties, Al Jolson's career declined temporarily.

It wasn't until 1946 when Columbia Pictures filmed his biography, *The Jolson Story*, that the great performer made his return—this time by writing "Anniversary Song" with collaborator Saul Chaplin. Within a few months, the song topped the Hit Parade and has become a musical classic, permanently linked with the memory of Al Jolson.

Al Jolson

ANNIVERSARY SONG

Words and Music by
AL JOLSON and
SAUL CHAPLIN
Based on a theme by Ivanovici

Moderately

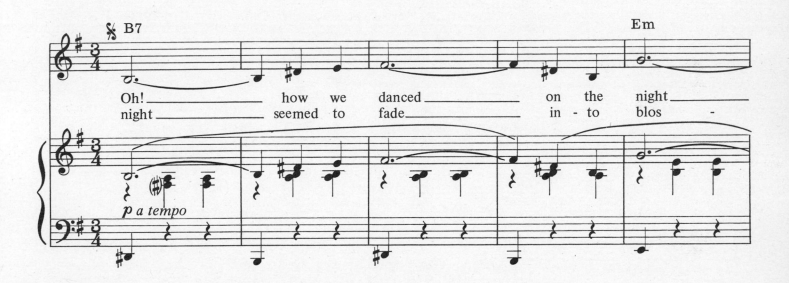

Oh! how we danced on the night we were wed, We vowed our true

night seemed to fade in-to blos - som-ing dawn, The sun shone a -

love _____ though a word _____ was-n't said. _____
new _____ but the dance _____ lin-gered on. _____

___ The world _____ was in bloom, _____ there were
___ Could we _____ but re-live _____ that sweet

stars _____ in the skies, _____ Ex-cept _____
mo - ment sub-lime, _____ We'd find _____

___ for the few _____ that were there _____
___ that our love _____ is un-al -

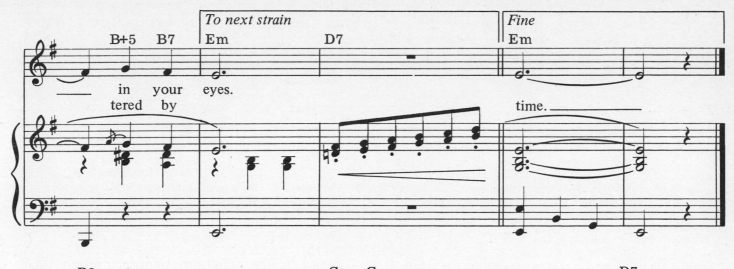

in your eyes.
tered by

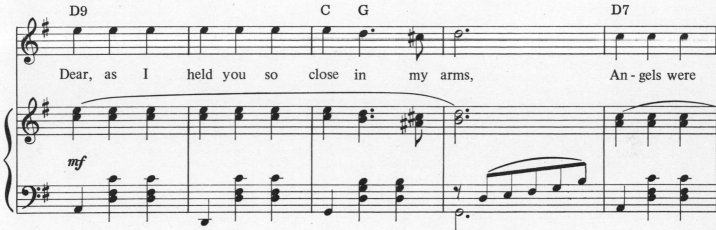

Dear, as I held you so close in my arms, An-gels were

sing-ing a hymn to your charms, Two hearts gent-ly beat-ing were

mur-mur-ing low, "My dar-ling, I love you so." _____ The

Other Songs Identified With Entertainers

NIGHT AND DAY

Verse
Like the beat, beat, beat of the tom-tom, when the jungle shadows fall;
Like the tick, tick, tock of the stately clock, as it stands against the wall;
Like the drip, drip, drip of the raindrops when summer show'r is through;
So a voice within me keeps repeating, you, you, you.

Chorus
Night And Day you are the one,
Only you beneath the moon and under the sun.
Whether near to me or far, it's no matter, darling, where you are,
I think of you Night And Day.
Day and night, why is it so
That this longing for you follows wherever I go?
In the roaring traffic's boom, in the silence of my lonely room,
I think of you, Night And Day!
Night And Day under the hide of me
There's an oh, such a hungry yearning burning inside of me.
And its torment won't be through
'Til you let me spend my life making love to you,
Day and night, Night And Day.

Words and Music by Cole Porter

© Copyright 1932 by Harms, Inc. Copyright renewed 1947.

SWEET ELOISE

Sweet Eloise, sing the birds in the trees,
When she is near, you can hear them singing sweet melodies,
They're just for my Eloise.
Sweet Eloise is a beautiful sight,
Ole Mister Moon comes around to look at her ev'ry night,
Her smile's a warm summer breeze, the smile of Eloise.
And tho' there may be clouds in the skies,
There's always sunshine deep in her eyes.
In case you didn't know, roses grow, hopin' some day
They'll be pressed and caressed in her bouquet.
Sweet Eloise is so lovely to love,
You will agree she's the only girl that you're dreamin' of.
But you'll be wastin' your time,
'Cause Eloise is all mine.

Words by Mack David   Music by Russ Morgan

© Copyright 1942 by Shapiro, Bernstein & Co. Copyright renewed.

IF YOU KNEW SUSIE

Verse 1
I have got a sweetie known as Susie,
In the words of Shakespeare she's a "wow,"
Though all of you
May know her, too,
I'd like to shout right now:

Chorus 1
If You Knew Susie like I know Susie,
Oh! Oh!
Oh! What a girl!
There's none so classy as this fair lassie,
Oh! Oh!
Holy Moses! What a chassis!
We went riding,
She didn't balk,
Back from Yonkers
I'm the one that had to walk!
If You Knew Susie like I know Susie,
Oh! Oh! What a girl!

Verse 2
Susie has a perfect reputation,
No one ever saw her on a spree,
Nobody knows
Where Susie goes,
Nobody knows but me:

Chorus 2
If You Knew Susie like I know Susie,
Oh! Oh!
Oh! What a girl!
She wears long tresses and nice tight dresses,
Oh! Oh!
What a future she possesses!
Out in public
How she can yawn,
In a parlor
You would think the war was on!
If You Knew Susie Like I know Susie,
Oh! Oh! What a girl!

Words and Music by B. G. DeSylva and Joseph Meyer

© Copyright 1925 Shapiro, Bernstein & Co. Copyright renewed.

THAT'S MY DESIRE

To spend one night with you
In our old rendezvous,
And reminisce with you,
That's My Desire.

To meet where gypsies play
Down in that dim cafe,
And dance 'till break of day,
That's My Desire.

We'll sip a little glass of wine,
I'll gaze into your eyes divine.
I'll feel the touch of your lips pressing on mine.

To hear you whisper low
Just when it's time to go,
"Cherie, I love you so,"
That's My Desire.

Words by Carroll Loveday   Music by Helmy Kreso
© Copyright 1931 by Mills Music, Inc. Copyright renewed 1959.

SECRET LOVE

Verse
Nobody knew, not even you,
When I first started walking on wings;
But how long can a man or woman ever hope to hide
Love that's locked up inside?
Ev'ry story worth the spinning
Must have a beginning.

Chorus
Once I had a Secret Love
That lived within the heart of me,
All too soon my Secret Love
Became impatient to be free,
So I told a friendly star,
The way that dreamers often do,
Just how wonderful you are
And why I'm so in love with you.
Now I shout it from the highest hills,
Even told the golden daffodils;
At last my heart's an open door,
And my secret love's no secret any more.

Words by Paul Francis Webster   Music by Sammy Fain
© Copyright 1953 by Remick Music Corp. Copyright renewed.

NATURE BOY

There was a boy, a very strange, enchanted boy;
They say he wandered very far, very far over land and sea.
A little shy and sad of eye,
But very wise was he.
And then one day, one magic day he passed my way,
And as we spoke of many things, fools and kings, this he said to me:
"The greatest thing you'll ever learn
Is just to love and be loved in return."

Words and Music by Eden Abba
© Copyright 1948 by Crestview Music Corp.
Sole selling agent: Ivan Mogull Music Corporation

PAPER DOLL

Verse
I guess I've had a million dolls or more,
I guess I've played the doll game o'er and o'er,
I just quarreled with Sue, that's why I'm blue;
She's gone away and left me just like all dolls do.
I'll tell you boys it's tough to be alone,
And it's tough to love a doll that's not your own.
I'm thru with all of them, I'll never fall again,
'Cause this is what I'll do:

Chorus
I'm goin' to buy a Paper Doll that I can call my own,
A doll that other fellows cannot steal.
And then the flirty, flirty guys with their flirty, flirty eyes,
Will have to flirt with dollies that are real.
When I come home at night she will be waiting,
She'll be the truest doll in all this world.
I'd rather have a Paper Doll to call my own,
Than have a fickle-minded real live girl.

Words and Music by Johnny S. Black
© Copyright 1930 by Edward B. Marks Music Co. Copyright 1943.

INKA DINKA DOO

Ink-a Dink-a Doo,
A dink-a dee, A dink-a doo.
Oh, what a tune for crooning,
Ink-a Dink-a Doo,
A dink-a dee, A dink-a doo;
It's got the whole world spooning.
Eskimo bells up in Iceland
Are ringing, they've made their own Paradise Land,
Singing Ink-a Dink-a Doo,
A dink-a dee, A dink-a doo,
Simply means Ink-a Dink-a Dee, A Dink-a Doo.

Words and Music by Jimmie "Schnozzle" Durante, Ben Ryan, and Harry Donnelly
© Copyright 1933 by Bourne Co., New York, N.Y. Copyright renewed.

Sing-Along Songs

Beneath every raspy, out-of-tune voice is the soul of a Caruso or a Jenny Lind. Though few people have the talent and training to become famous performers, almost everyone has the desire to sing. And for the most part, everyone does sing, even if it's limited to the shower. For these shower singers and for the timid tenors and barroom baritones of the world, there's sing-along music. You don't need to be a soloist to be included. If there's safety in numbers, the mere number of average-to-awful voices that make up any sing-along group gives everyone courage to relax and have fun.

Ever since the earliest days of parlor pianos and family songfests, group singing has retained its immense popularity. The first public appearances of the sing-along phenomenon may have been about the time of musical short features in movie theaters where the audience was invited to "follow the bouncing ball" and sing well-known favorites. Only the faint of heart left for the lobby—the rest of the people stayed and joined in with voices that ranged from tremulous to tumultuous.

Then, in the 1950s, a talented bearded gentleman took sing-along another step by capturing the same spirit of fun around a piano and creating a musical fun-for-all on television. Mitch Miller's sing-along sessions became regular family entertainment. And on into the sixties, the younger generation still hadn't stopped singing—only this time the accompaniment was a guitar.

Though times change, the spirit of sing-alongs and the music that is sung seem to go on forever. The same bouncy music that rocked Grandmother's living room is still generating fun-filled excitement today. What's the common denominator? It's the honest-to-goodness singability of these songs. Start with a melodic tune, add old-fashioned harmony and some lyrics that grab you in your sentimental spot, and you've got the formula for sing-along music. It's fun, it's informal, it's enthusiastic, and it's American through and through.

On the following pages you'll find words and music to some of the most often sung and most harmonically mutilated songs that have ever brought a gang of people together around a piano. Here are everyone's favorite oldies but goodies.

Love was a national pastime in America in the early 1900s. When women weren't reading romantic fiction, they were daydreaming about the blessed state of matrimony. So, it was only natural that a song such as "Let Me Call You Sweetheart" would become a hit from East Coast to West.

Writers Beth Whitson and Leo Friedman created this successful love ballad in 1910—when women swathed themselves in yards of elegant fabric and donned feathered headdresses that could rival any aviary's plumage. Women were meant to be loved, expected to be loved, and were disappointed if their lives were without a dashing hero of the type that surrounded the popular Gibson Girl. Literature, art, drama, and of course, popular music played into the hands of the romanticists.

However, this period was not all love notes and tokens of affection. In San Francisco the Board of Censors clamped down on 32 motion picture releases as "unfit for public exhibition," and one vaudeville troupe billed as "America's Worst Act" actually had to perform behind a net to protect the group from offerings of fruit and vegetables that were heaped upon them.

In this period of paradox—the sweet innocence of romance and the breaking out of the traditional mold—America produced some memorable entertainment and some equally memorable music.

LET ME CALL YOU SWEETHEART

(I'm In Love With You)

Words by
BETH SLATER WHITSON

Music by
LEO FRIEDMAN

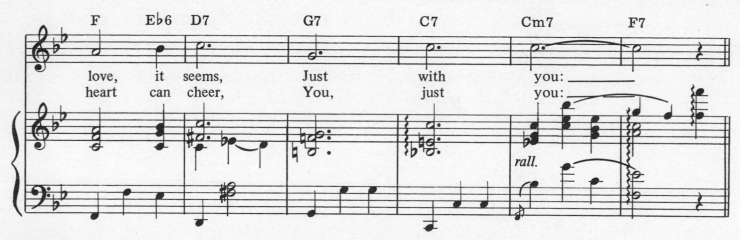

Let me hear you whis-per that you love me,

too. _____ Keep the love - light glow-ing in your eyes

so true, _____ Let Me Call You Sweet - heart,

I'm in love with you. you. _____

Had you lived in the 1890s, you might well have heard your popular music at a saloon. Sometimes these places would have a couple of musicians, sometimes an entire orchestra, and sometimes just a piano. Vocals were supplied by singing waiters or by the establishment's own star. At the Atlantic Gardens in New York, for example, a lady named Jessie Lindsay was stirring them up with her trademark song, "A Bicycle Built For Two." And at the Abbey, another popular haunt, people would come in droves to hear Maude Nugent sing "Sweet Rosie O'Grady."

There is speculation that Maude's husband, songwriter William Jerome, had a hand in "Rosie's" creation, and that may be true, for she never wrote another successful song. There's no doubt, though, that Maude was the one who took it to a publisher—and was almost turned down.

"There are just too many girls' names titles on the market," he said. "It won't sell." Maude disagreed. She snatched the music off the piano, stomped off, and headed for another publisher. With this, the publisher abruptly changed his mind and decided to buy the piece. It is one of the ironies of the song business that he made a fortune on it. Maude was paid only $100.

SWEET ROSIE O'GRADY

Words and Music by
MAUDE NUGENT

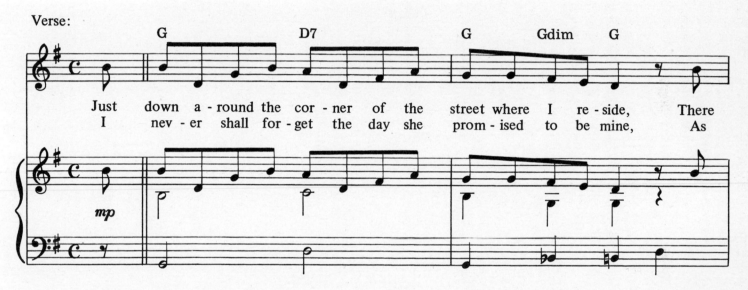

Verse:

Just down a-round the cor-ner of the street where I re-side, There
I nev-er shall for-get the day she prom-ised to be mine, As

lives the cut-est lit-tle girl that I have ev-er spied. Her
we sat tell-ing love-tales in the gold-en sum-mer time. 'Twas

name is Rose O' Gra - dy and I don't mind tell - ing you, That
on her fin - ger that I placed a small en - gage - ment ring, While

she's the sweet - est lit - tle Rose the gar - den ev - er grew.
in the trees the lit - tle birds this song they seemed to sing:

rall.

Moderate waltz

Chorus:

Sweet Ros - ie O' Gra - dy, My dear lit - tle

Rose,_____ She's my stead - y la - dy,

Most ev' - ry - one knows, _____ And when we are

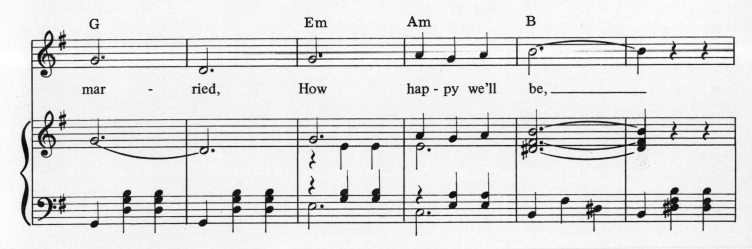

mar - ried, How hap - py we'll be, _____

I love Sweet Ros - ie O' Gra - dy, And Ros - ie O'

Gra - dy loves me. me. _____

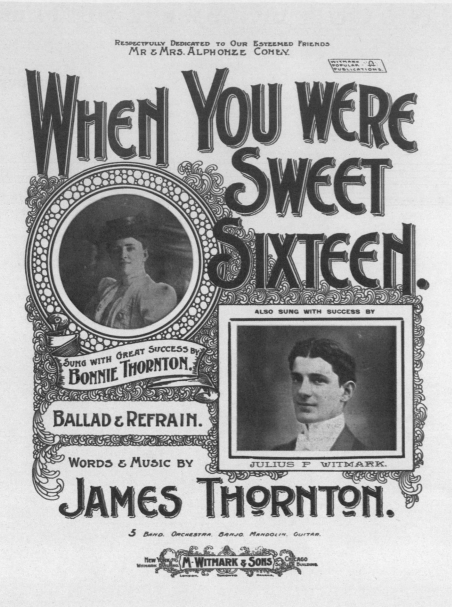

There's not a wife in the world who hasn't at some time or other asked her husband if he still loved her. Bonnie Thornton was no exception. She had reason to ask, too, because almost every night during the 1890s her husband James and his favorite drinking companion, fighter John L. Sullivan, could be found making the rounds of New York's saloons and boozily swearing their friendship until dawn. And when Thornton wasn't out with Sullivan, he'd be using up his advances with other pals, which naturally was upsetting to Bonnie.

In one of his more serious moments, Thornton did tell Bonnie what she needed to hear when he said, "I love you like I did when you were sweet sixteen." This expression of affection also inspired "When You Were Sweet Sixteen."

The year was 1898. Bonnie Thornton introduced her husband's song in vaudeville, and before long the sheet music sales topped the million mark. Much later on—1947 to be exact—the million mark was set again, this time by Perry Como's recording of it.

"When You Were Sweet Sixteen" is a nostalgic part of America's musical history. It has all of the old-fashioned charm and sweetness that we like to associate with the turn of the century, and it has the harmony that always will be associated with sing-along music.

WHEN YOU WERE SWEET SIXTEEN

Words and Music by
JAMES THORNTON

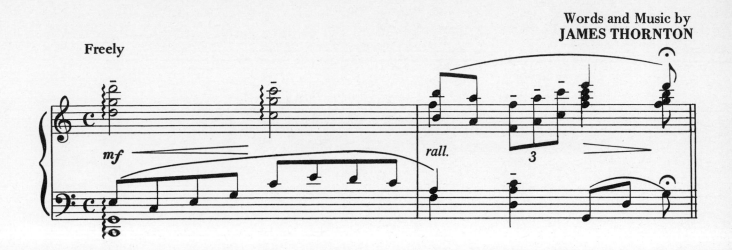

Verse:

When first I saw the love-light in your eye,＿＿＿＿＿＿ I
Last night I dreamt I held your hand in mine,＿＿＿＿＿＿ And

dreamt the world held naught but joy for me.＿＿＿＿＿＿ And
once a-gain you were my hap-py bride.＿＿＿＿＿＿ I

green. _____ Come to me or my dream of love is

o'er, _____ I love you as I loved you,

When you were sweet, _____ When You Were Sweet Six-

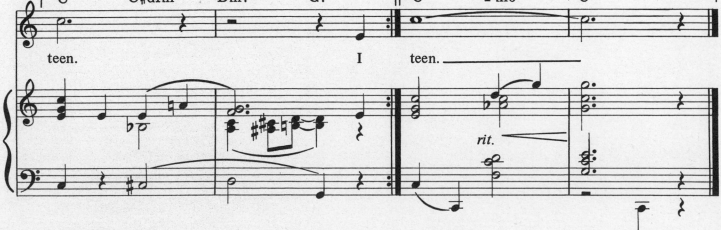

teen. I teen.

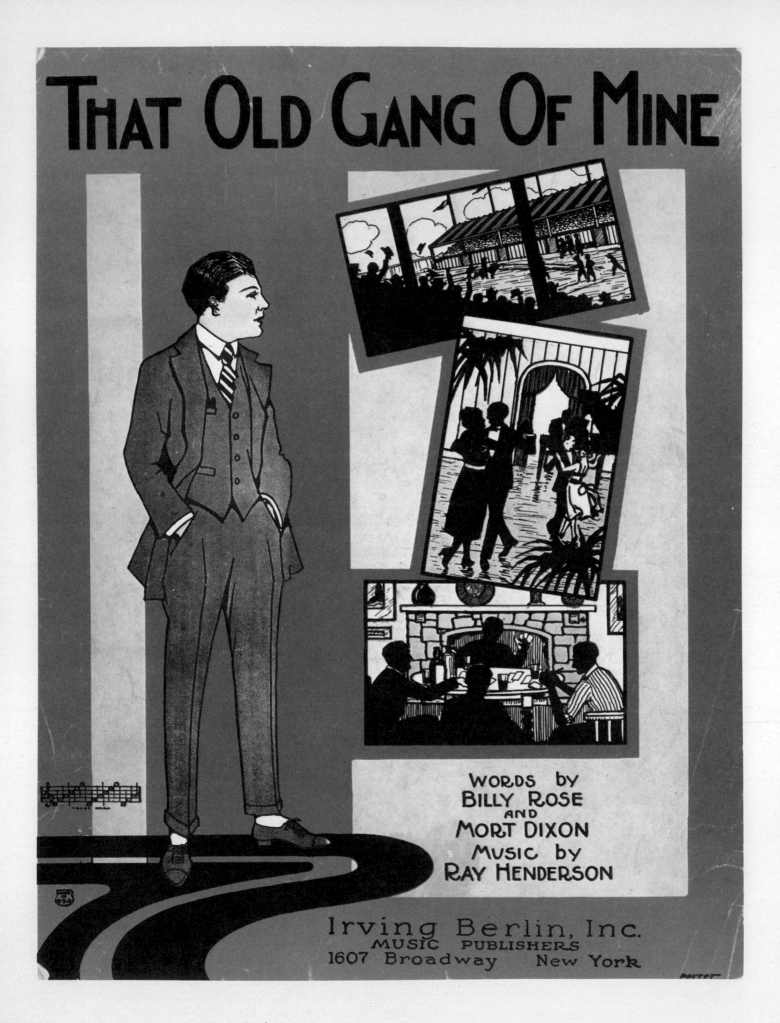

THAT OLD GANG OF MINE

WORDS BY
BILLY ROSE
AND
MORT DIXON
MUSIC BY
RAY HENDERSON

Irving Berlin, Inc.
MUSIC PUBLISHERS
1607 Broadway   New York

That Old Gang of Mine

"That Old Gang Of Mine" was the turning point for its young
lyricist Billy Rose, who eventually became one of
the richest men on Broadway. When he was a young child, though,
sometimes all his family had to eat was a loaf of
stale bread. And when the rent couldn't be paid, the children
in the family would sleep in the streets. Billy
decided then and there that he was going to be rich. He didn't
start out in songwriting—but with shorthand.

After taking lessons from Robert Gregg himself, Rose took
the world title for speed and had learned to take
shorthand both forwards and backwards with either hand. Soon,
he was at the War Industries Board sitting in on conferences
of important industrialists who lived the way he wanted to live.

He might have stayed there, and "That Old Gang of
Mine" might never have been written and introduced in the
Ziegfeld *Follies* in 1923 had it not been for a friend's
chance remark that songwriters made $75,000 a year. On hearing
this, Billy trotted off to the library and waded through
volumes of the popular songs of the last half-century trying
to figure out what made the good ones click.

Before long, he was pestering Tin Pan Alley pianists to put
his lyrics to music. Just to get rid of Billy, a fellow
named Irving Bibo wrote the music for "Ain't Nature Grand,"
which brought in $5000. Rose did well with two more
songs, too, but it wasn't until "That Old Gang Of Mine," with
Mort Dixon helping out on the lyrics and Ray Henderson
doing the music, that Billy Rose started sharing in the "good
life." Among other things, he rented a luxuriously
furnished apartment, hired a Chinese chef, and purchased a fancy
racing car for drives around town.

THAT OLD GANG OF MINE

Words by
BILLY ROSE
and **MORT DIXON**

Music by
RAY HENDERSON

Slowly

Verse:

I've got a long - in' way down in my heart,___
Last night I strolled to that old neigh - bor - hood,___

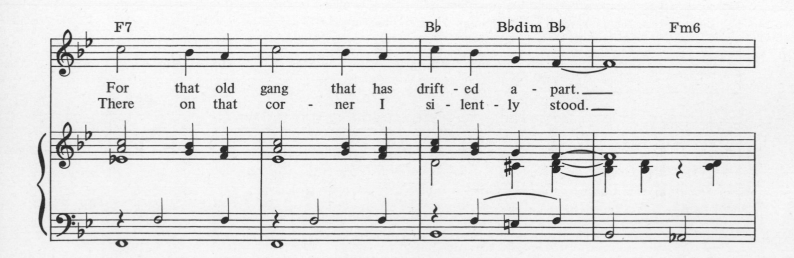

For that old gang that has drift - ed a - part.___
There on that cor - ner I si - lent - ly stood.___

They were the best pals that I ev - er had, ____
I felt so blue as the crowds hur - ried by, ____

I nev - er thought that I'd want them so bad. ____
No - bod - y knew how I want - ed to cry. ____

poco a poco rit.

Chorus:

Gee, but I'd give the world to see That

mf *a tempo*

bye   for - ev - er,   old   fel - lows   and   gals, ___   Good -

bye   for - ev - er,   old   sweet - hearts   and   pals. ___   (God   bless   them.)

Gee,   but I'd give the world   to   see   That   Old

Gang   Of   Mine.   Mine. ___

In the Good Old Summertime

Ever wondered what the good old summertime was like in 1902 when this song first made its appearance?
Summer meant wearing scratchy wool bathing suits at the beach, picnicking in the park, drinking fresh-squeezed
lemonade out of galvanized washtubs, playing lawn tennis, touring in an open car (providing you had a duster
to protect your clothes from road hazards), or taking in a minstrel show.

Summer was a fun time. On one particularly fine day back then, George Evans, a popular songwriter/minstrel
of the day, was picnicking at Brighton Beach, near New York City's Coney Island, with a friend of his named Ren
Shields and a popular vaudeville singer by the name of Blanche Ring. "Ah," said Evans, leaning back and taking in the
balmy sea air, "there's nothing quite like the good old summertime."

On hearing this comment, Shields, who was always open to inspiration, said he thought that this would be a great
song title. When he got back to New York, he made up the words. A few days later, he and Evans were together
again, and the famous minstrel began working out the tune.

Blanche Ring got into the act, too, making plans to add the new song to her next show, *The Defender*, which was
to open soon in Boston. During rehearsals, there had been a runway sticking into the orchestra, and Blanche got the
idea of hiring a gang of Harvard students to sit near by and sing along as she paraded down the runway. The chorus
and the runway were such novelties that the new song received a great amount of attention. The runway stayed a part
of musical revues after that—and "In The Good Old Summertime" has remained a favorite ever since.

IN THE GOOD OLD SUMMERTIME

Words by
REN SHIELDS

Music by
GEORGE EVANS

Good old sum - mer time,_____ When your day's work is
Good old sum - mer time,_____ Those days full of

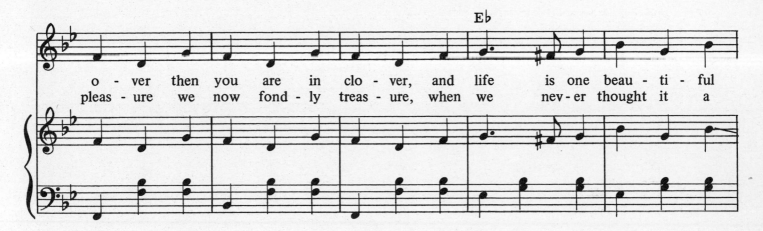

o - ver then you are in clo - ver, and life is one beau - ti - ful
pleas - ure we now fond - ly treas - ure, when we nev - er thought it a

rhyme,_____ No trou - ble an - noy - ing, each one is en -
crime_____ To go steal - ing cher - ries, with face brown as

joy - ing, The good old sum - mer time._____
ber - ries,____ Good old sum - mer time._____

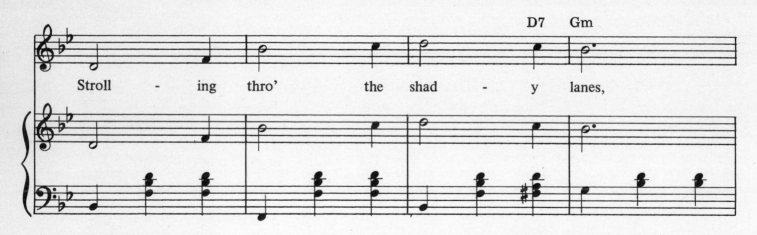

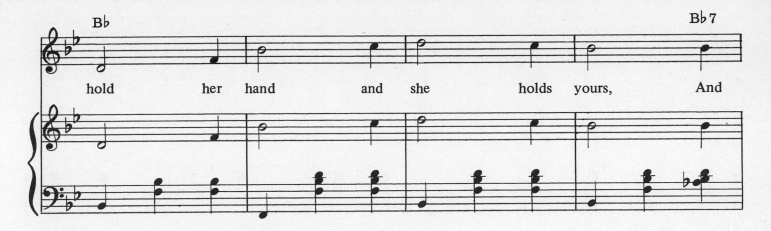

hold her hand and she holds yours, And

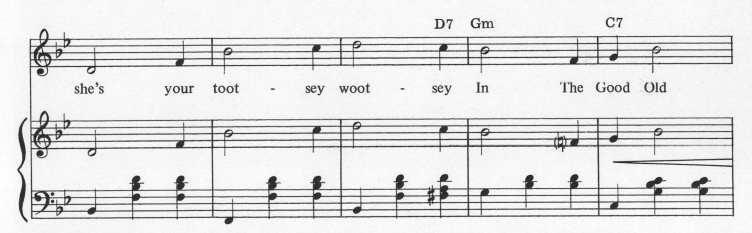

that's a ver - y good sign _____ That

she's your toot - sey woot - sey In The Good Old

Sum - mer Time. _____ In The Time. _____

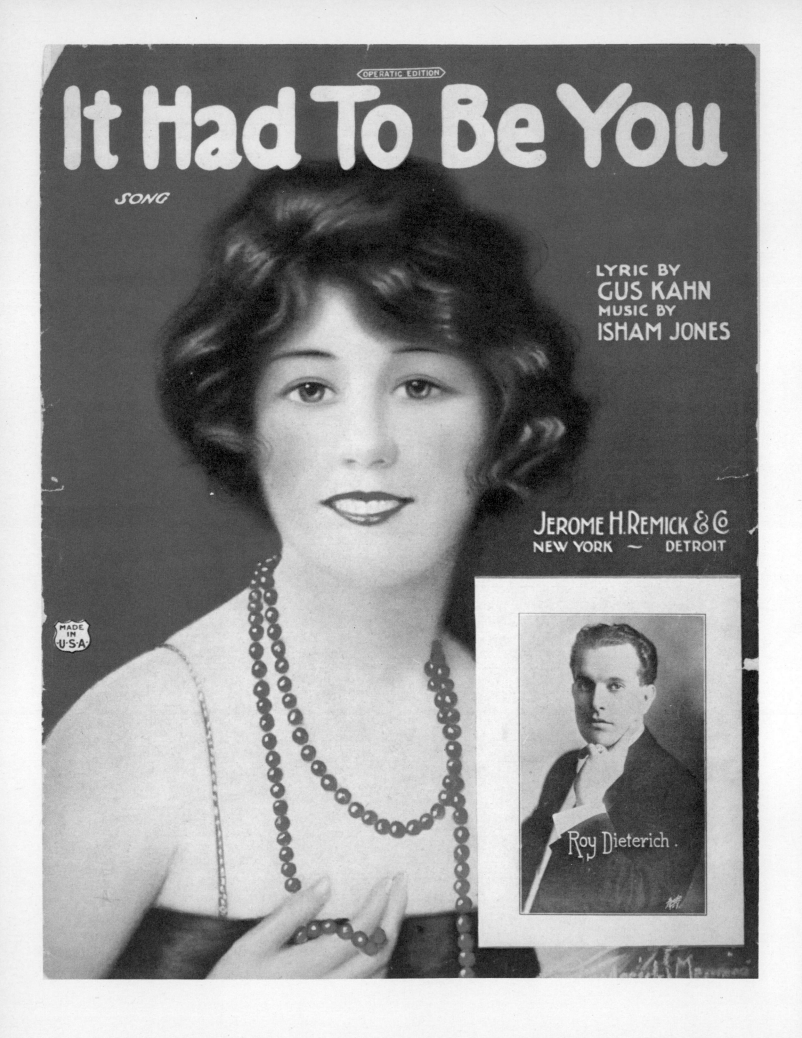

It Had To Be You

The Isham Jones-Gus Kahn song "It Had To Be You" couldn't have made its debut at a better time than in 1924, when America was just about at the height of the dance craze that nearly turned the country's social life upside-down.

Polkas and waltzes had given way to the shimmy, the Charleston, and a dance called the black bottom, which was supposed to suggest the way you would drag your feet through the Suwannee River mud. Restaurants were judged on the quality of their music, and tea rooms and hotels hired hostesses to dance with businessmen who wanted to practice on their lunch hours. The *Ladies' Home Journal*, the Pope, and ministers decried the mania, and when one couple broke their ankles doing the tango, nay-sayers said that besides being immoral, dancing was dangerous.

Bandleaders, of course, were much in demand, and they had the power to make or break songs. Isham Jones was one of the best, so he could give his compositions the needed exposure. His first hit, "Swingin' Down The Lane," was followed by "I'll See You In My Dreams" and "It Had To Be You."

Every song falls from the pinnacle sooner or later, though, and "It Had To Be You" was no exception. Isham Jones retired when the Depression put cover charges out of the range of most dancers' pocketbooks, but his music didn't disappear. In the forties, when a war-weary song business was casting about for oldies-but-goodies to revive, "It Had To Be You" found its way onto many Hollywood soundtracks, starting with the 1943 film *Is Everybody Happy?* Then, in 1945, Betty Hutton sang it in *Incendiary Blonde*, and Danny Thomas lent it his interpretation in the 1951 film version of Gus Kahn's biography, *I'll See You In My Dreams.*

IT HAD TO BE YOU

Words by
GUS KAHN

Music by
ISHAM JONES

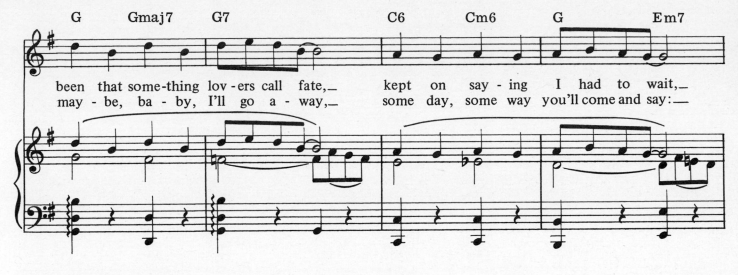

but they would-n't do,_____ For no-bod-y else

gave me a thrill,__ With all your faults__ I love you still,__

It Had To Be You,__ won-der-ful you,__ had to be you.__

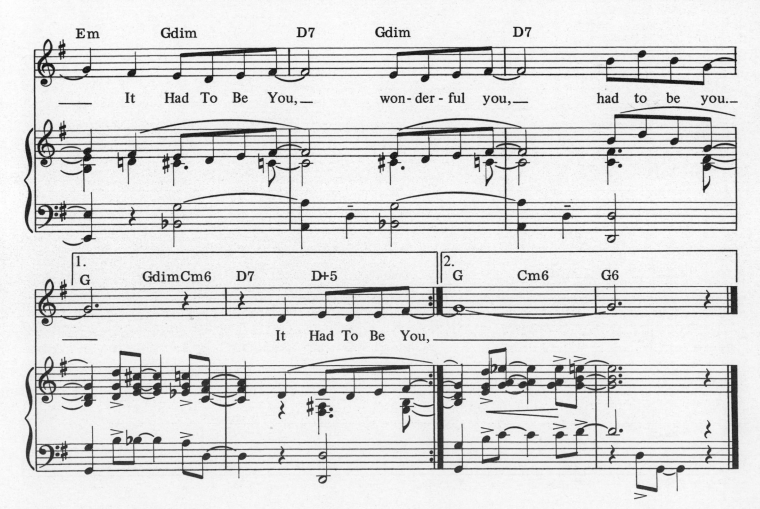

It Had To Be You,_____

When Sunny Clapp wrote "Girl Of My Dreams," little did he know
he was writing a tribute to every girl who has ever been loved, admired, or elected
sweetheart of a fraternity. The Sigma Chi's had a sweetheart song,
but with the composition of "Girl Of My Dreams," every fraternity on every
campus in the United States had a song to dedicate to their sweethearts.

In 1927, when "Girl Of My Dreams" was published, campus life was a montage
of ukuleles and hip flasks, cloche hats, and rolled stockings. The way
to get from one party to another was in a flivver, and any flapper that was pretty
was considered "the cat's meow" or "the bee's knees." Though
students liked to think of themselves as unconventional, they were all anxious
to join a fraternity, and the "Greeks" were in their heyday.

With a piano in every fraternity house and pretty girls on every campus,
it's easy to see why "Girl Of My Dreams" got off to such a flying start.
And today's college songfests are just as likely to bring out the harmony of Sunny
Clapp's tune as those of the twenties were. As long as there are girls—
and men to dream about them—and as long as there are sing-alongs, someone
will always request "Girl Of My Dreams."

GIRL OF MY DREAMS

Words and Music by
SUNNY CLAPP

Dear, it seems years since we part - ed,
It's strange how life deals you sor - row,

Years full of tears and re - gret;
Sun - shine and joy al - ways nigh;

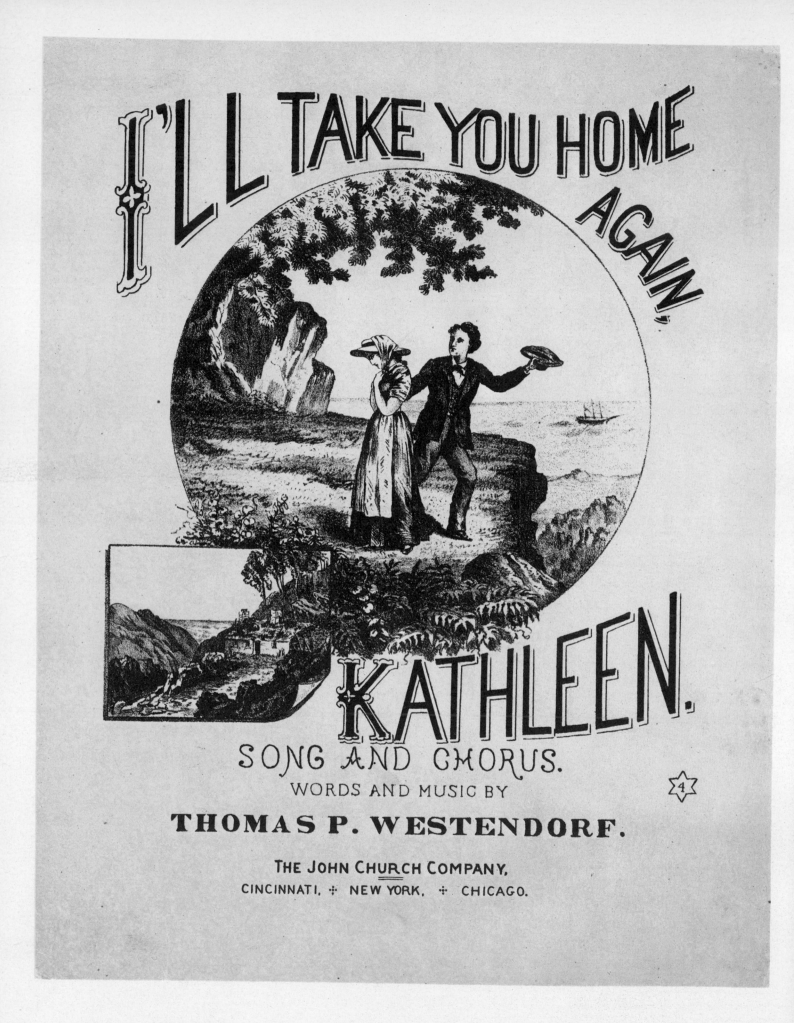

I'll Take You Home Again, Kathleen

When you read the words of "I'll Take You Home Again, Kathleen" (the first of a series of sentimental ballads that appeared in the latter part of the 1800s), it's easy enough to mourn right along with the composer, Thomas Westendorf, and to believe the legend that has grown up about the song. That story tells of a young married couple whose baby has just been buried. The husband takes his wife, Kathleen, to Europe in hopes that the trip somehow will help her forget the pain and the sorrow. Alas, it will not be stilled. In the middle of Germany, she's suddenly overwhelmed by her misery. "I must go home," the lady sighs, so she and her husband board the first ship leaving for home. But her melancholy saps her strength, and her slender hold on life has been loosened by the time the vessel gets back to the United States. After this, all the young widower has left is his poems and his lachrymose songs.

Every morsel of this tale was taken as gospel until, in the 1940s, an enterprising researcher at the Library of Congress took the matter into his competent hands and showed that the legend that had brought tears to the eyes of thousands of people ever since 1876 had about as much truth in it as a politician's campaign speech. What actually happened was far more prosaic than this.

Very simply, Thomas Paine Westendorf, a Virginia-born schoolteacher, had to stay home in Plainfield, Indiana, and look after his pupils while his wife went to visit relatives in Ogdensburg, New York, shortly after their marriage. Thomas did miss his wife, though, and it was loneliness that prompted "I'll Take You Home Again, Kathleen."

I'LL TAKE YOU HOME AGAIN, KATHLEEN

Arranged by Frank Metis

Words and Music by
THOMAS P. WESTENDORF

Moderately slow

Though the polka is danced all over America, it's not a traditional American dance by any means. Still, there's nothing more American than the song "Beer Barrel Polka." The English language version of this well-known Czechoslovakian tune, written in 1939 by Lew Brown, reinforces the fondness that Americans have for their foreign heritages.

Soon after "Beer Barrel Polka" made its debut as an American song, it swept the country by storm. And this was the country that was dancing the Big Apple, doing the Lindy Hop, and "truckin'," which was the jive talk label for a finger-waving, hip-tossing walk particularly contagious among teen-agers.

This was also the Swing Era, when "jiving-it-up" was the popular thing to be doing, yet a simple little polka adapted from a foreign melody soared to popularity, passing up a lot of typically all-American songs.

"Beer Barrel Polka" was made a hit with the renditions of Sammy Kaye, the Andrews Sisters, and other top-flight performers of the time. During the Second World War, American troops carried the sprightly song all over the world.

From USO canteens to fraternity beer parties, "Beer Barrel Polka" is as much a part of the music as beer is part of the refreshments.

BEER BARREL POLKA
(Roll Out the Barrel)

Words and Music by
**LEW BROWN,
WLADIMIR A. TIMM,
VASEK ZEMAN**
and **JAROMIR VEJVODA**

Polka

Verse:

There's a gar - den, what a gar - den, On - ly hap - py fa - ces bloom there, And there's

nev - er an - y room there For a wor - ry or a gloom there. Oh, there's

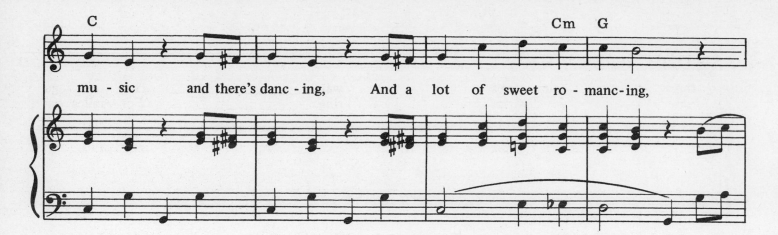

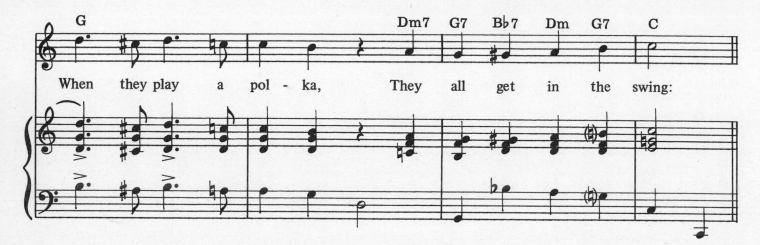

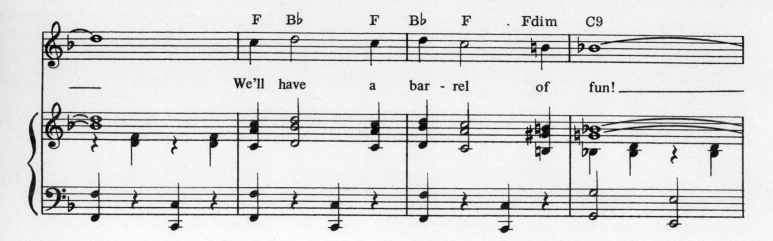

We'll have a bar-rel of fun!

Roll out the bar-rel,

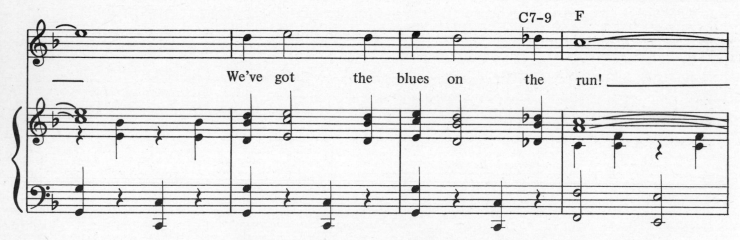

We've got the blues on the run!

Zing! Boom! Ta-rar-rel!

When Irish Eyes are Smiling
Chauncey Olcott's
Song Successes
in his
New Production
THE
ISLE O'DREAMS
BY RIDA JOHNSON YOUNG
DIRECTION OF MR. HENRY MILLER
CALLING OF THE SEA, THE 60
By Geo. Graff, Jr., Chauncey Olcott and Ernest R. Ball
ISLE O' DREAMS 60
By Geo. Graff, Jr., Chauncey Olcott and Ernest R. Ball
KATHLEEN AROON 60
By Louis Weslyn, Chauncey Olcott and Ernest R. Ball
MOTHER MACHREE 60
By Rida Johnson Young, Chauncey Olcott and Ernest R. Ball
WHEN IRISH EYES ARE SMILING . 60
By Geo. Graff, Jr., Chauncey Olcott and Ernest R. Ball
INSTRUMENTAL
SELECTION 1.00
M. WITMARK & SONS
NEW YORK - CHICAGO - SAN FRANCISCO - LONDON - PARIS - MELBOURNE

Chauncey Olcott

When Irish Eyes Are Smiling

Ernest Ball wrote many songs before anybody ever heard about him. So, it's probable that "When Irish Eyes Are Smiling" would be gathering dust on some music publisher's shelf had it not been for the stroke of luck that made him famous.

The young man came to New York in 1890 looking for fame and fortune, but after almost 10 years in the city he was still only a publisher's pianist, making twenty dollars a week. Life seemed to be at a standstill until one day a dapper Irish-American appeared in his office. James J. Walker was later a New York mayor and a state senator, but just then his head was full of lyrics. In his pocket he had what he thought were good ones, and he wanted Ball to write the music. Ball read over the lines and said he'd think it over.

The result, "Will You Love Me In December As You Did In May?", and the next songs he wrote were such hits that Buffalo-born Chauncey Olcott, the most famous "Irish" tenor of his day, approached him to collaborate on a series of Irish ballads. "When Irish Eyes Are Smiling" was introduced in the 1912 musical *The Isle O' Dreams*. Olcott, working with Rida Johnson Young, also helped on the lyrics to "Mother Machree," a song that was basic to the repertoire of another popular Irish tenor, John McCormack, who mourned Ball's death in 1927. "Ernie Ball is not dead," he said. "He will live forever in his songs."

The secret to the success of Ball's Irish songs was his talent for writing from the heart. "If the sentiment is straight and true," said Ball, "the song has a chance. Talk about a man's home, his wife, his mother, or his children and you have his ear." It was a lesson Ernest Ball learned early in his long and successful career.

WHEN IRISH EYES ARE SMILING

Lyric by
CHAUNCEY OLCOTT
& GEO. GRAFF Jr.

Music by
ERNEST R. BALL

D B7 E7 A D A7
stone you'd be - guile, So there's nev - er a tear-drop should fall. When your
all the day long, Comes your laugh-ter so ten - der and light. For the
D A7 D
sweet lilt - ing laugh - ter's like some fair - y song, And your eyes twin - kle
spring-time of life is the sweet-est of all, There is ne'er a real
D7 G E7
ten.
bright as can be; You should laugh all the while and all
care or re - gret; And while spring-time is ours through-out
ten.

oth - er times smile, And now smile— a smile for me._____
all of youth's hours, Let us smile— each chance we get._____

Chorus:

When I - rish Eyes Are Smil - ing,_____ Sure it's like a
morn in Spring._____ In the lilt of I - rish
laugh - ter, You can hear the an - gels sing._____

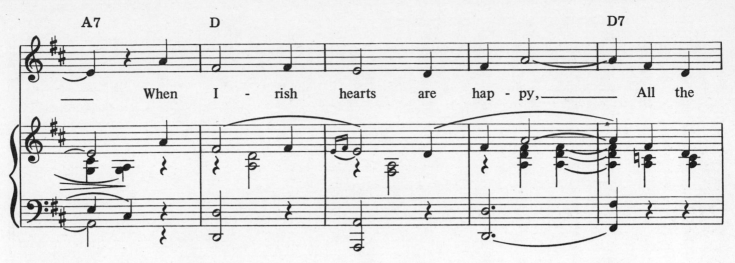

When I - rish hearts are hap - py, _____ All the

world seems bright and gay, _____ And When I - rish

Eyes Are Smil - ing, Sure they steal__ your heart a -

way. When way. _____

Lillian Lorraine, one of the great female stars of vaudeville, made the Gus Edwards-
Edward Madden tune "By The Light Of The Silvery Moon" her signature
song starting in 1909, the year it was introduced in Edward's *School Boys And
Girls*, a revue that featured children as singers, dancers, comedians,
and mimics. Lillian picked it up from young Georgie Price, the revue's featured
performer. She performed the song on stage at the Ziegfeld's *Follies*
and kept on singing it to enthusiastic audiences everywhere until 1933.

That last run-through, at the festivities accompanying a theater opening, should
have been a happy occasion, and the all-star revue had attracted
an all-star audience. Gus Edwards, one of the on-stage stars, spotted Miss Lorraine
on the other side of the footlights and called her up to sing "By The
Light Of The Silvery Moon." But by then, the song was, at least for her, all wound
up with her long-gone youth and the great age of vaudeville, which
was on the outs. And Gus Edwards, who was almost a symbol of that era, was
rapidly becoming a show-business has-been. Vaudeville had been
so much a part of all their lives that it was sad to say good-bye, and when Lillian
Lorraine got past the first few bars, she broke down and cried.

BY THE LIGHT OF THE SILVERY MOON

Lyric by
ED. MADDEN

Music by
GUS EDWARDS

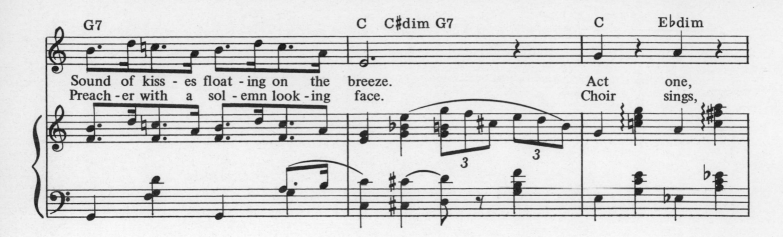

Sound of kiss - es float - ing on the breeze.
Preach - er with a sol - emn look - ing face.
Act one,
Choir sings,

be - gun
bell rings,
Di - a - logue, "Where would you like to spoon?"
Preach - er: "You are wed for - ev - er more."

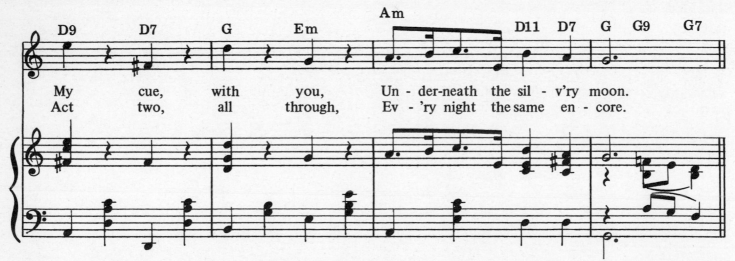

My cue, with you,
Act two, all through,
Un - der-neath the sil - v'ry moon.
Ev - 'ry night the same en - core.

Chorus:

By The Light_____ Of The Sil - ver-y Moon,_____ I want to

Home, Sweet Home

Homesickness is as universal an emotion as love—
and both emotions seem to generate appealing popular music.
In the case of "Home, Sweet Home," writer John Howard
Payne probably never suspected he was creating America's first
international hit. But he did. Something about the
poignancy of the lyrics and the plaintive melody went straight
to the heart of any American who had ever left home.

When Payne wrote "Home, Sweet Home" in 1823, he was
living in London, and his longing for America was so deep
that he had to find an outlet for it. Payne's homesickness gave
the world an unforgettable song. As a London musical
publication said after the song was published, "It is simple,
sweet, and touching beyond any air we have ever heard."

Payne's tribute to "home" was included in the opera *Clari,
Or, The Maid Of Milan* by Sir Henry Bishop, but it
gained its permanent fame through Jenny Lind, the incomparable
singer of the time who closed all of her performances
with "Home, Sweet Home." In 1859, seven years after John Howard
Payne had died, Miss Lind performed the number
in the White House.

By today's standards, the lyrics to "Home, Sweet Home"
might be considered pure schmaltz—and maybe they are.
But there seems to be a place for that kind of sincere expression
of an emotion, and in its own way, "Home, Sweet Home"
is more than a sing-along song. It's a tribute to a country that,
at the time of the song's creation, was less than
a half-century old. America has come a long way since that time,
but the song's sentiment is as true now as it was
then—"be it ever so humble, there's no place like home."

HOME, SWEET HOME

Arranged by Frank Metis

Words and Music by
JOHN HOWARD PAYNE
Sir **HENRY R. BISHOP**

2. I gaze on the moon as I tread the drear wild,
    And feel that my mother now thinks of her child;
    As she looks on that moon from our own cottage door,
    Thro' the woodbine whose fragrance shall cheer me no more.
    (Chorus)

3. An exile from home, splendor dazzles in vain,
    Oh, give me my lowly thatched cottage again;
    The birds singing gaily, that came at my call:
    Give me them and that peace of mind, dearer than all.
    (Chorus)

School Days

It was no accident that the Gus Edwards-Will Cobb song "School Days," introduced in 1909, became a hit in no time.
Edwards introduced the song in *School Boys And Girls*, which he wrote, directed, and starred in. He was cast as a schoolteacher in a room full of boys and girls who could sing, dance, and ham it up with a zest that audiences loved.
And when the little pupils put their classroom diligence behind "School Days," it headed for the musical honor roll, selling well in excess of three million copies of sheet music.

It was natural for Edwards to come up with this sort of act. He had been stage-crazy as a child, yet he wouldn't have made the big time were it not for some lucky breaks. The first came when vaudeville star Lottie Gilson adopted him as her singing stooge when she found him outside a stage door. In 1896, a vaudeville booking agent named James Hyde heard Edwards in a Brooklyn saloon and hired him as part of a quintet. After this, Edwards was on his way.

Later on, he became something of a legend because of his unerring nose for youthful talent. So assiduous a talent-hunter was he that theater men would say, "Pull in your kids! Here comes Gus Edwards!" whenever he was in town. Edwards discovered Ray Bolger, Georgie Jessel, Eleanor Powell, Georgie Price, Groucho Marx, and many others.

Edwards spent a few years in Hollywood in the late twenties and tried to make a Broadway comeback on his return. But by then, times had changed and children's acts never took hold the way they had before. In 1938 he retired to Los Angeles, where he died in 1945. But his most famous song lives on. "School Days" is perennial, not only with schoolchildren but with quartets and sing-along groups.

SCHOOL DAYS
(When We Were A Couple Of Kids)

Words by
WILL D. COBB

Music by
GUS EDWARDS

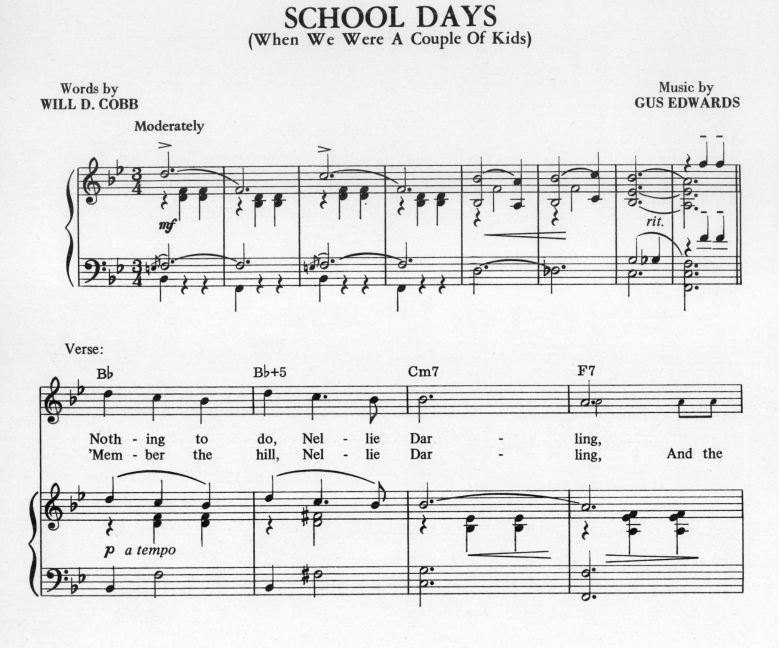

Verse:

Noth - ing to do, Nel - lie Dar - ling,
'Mem - ber the hill, Nel - lie Dar - ling, And the

Noth - ing to do, you say,_____
oak tree that grew on its brow?_____ They've

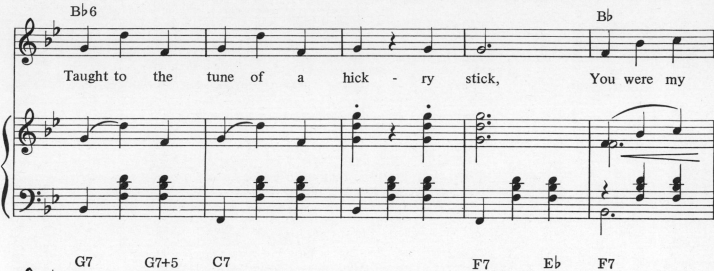

Taught to the tune of a hick - ry stick, You were my

queen in cal - i - co, I was your bash - ful

bare - foot beau, And you wrote on my slate, "I love you,

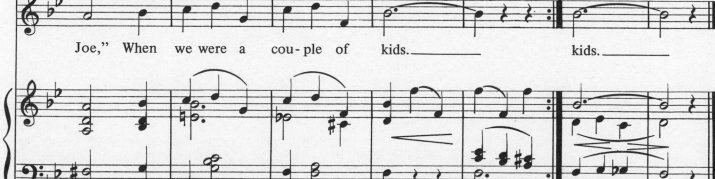

Joe," When we were a cou - ple of kids._____ kids._____

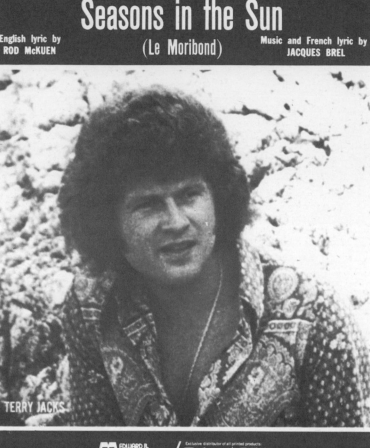

As recorded by TERRY JACKS on BELL

Seasons in the Sun
(Le Moribond)

English lyric by
ROD McKUEN

Music and French lyric by
JACQUES BREL

TERRY JACKS

EDWARD B. MARKS MUSIC CORPORATION / Belwin Mills Publishing Corp. MELVILLE, N.Y. 11746

MS 890

Price $1.25 in U.S.A.

"Seasons In The Sun" is the result of Rod McKuen's 1963 trip to Paris. That is where McKuen learned about the work of singer-composer Jacques Brel and adopted the relaxed French chansonnier style that he uses in concerts. McKuen, a composer and performer, also is the best-selling poet of the last 20 years.

McKuen attended school for only 4½ years because, as a child, he, his brother, and his mother moved from one western state to another for 11 years.

Later, when his mother remarried, McKuen ran away from home. From then on, he worked at odd jobs until he was hired as a disc jockey in his home town, Oakland, at age 17.

Back in the San Francisco Bay Area after a stint in the army, a colleague of his from the radio station, Phyllis Diller, set him up with a job singing intermission ballads at the Purple Onion, where he was discovered by a gossip columnist. She set him up in Hollywood, where he worked on four films before setting out for New York City, where he worked his way up from selling blood to giving so many concerts that doctors said he'd lose his voice if he didn't slow down.

Acting on this advice, McKuen started pouring out poetry, which soon was selling like hotcakes. Today, poet Rod McKuen is having his own season in the sun on the concert stages across the United States of America.

Rod McKuen

SEASONS IN THE SUN
(Le Moribond)

English Lyric by
ROD McKUEN

Music by
JACQUES BREL

Folk ballad style (moderato)

Chorus:

We had joy, we had fun, we had sea - sons in the sun; But the
joy, we had fun, we had sea - sons in the sun; But the
lives we had fun, we had sea - sons in the sun; But the

(to Fine last time)

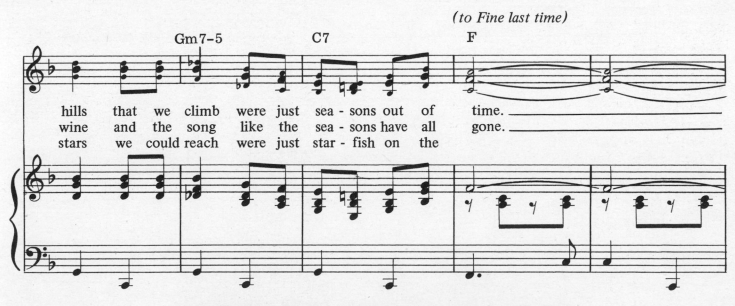

hills that we climb were just sea - sons out of time. _____
wine and the song like the sea - sons have all gone. _____
stars we could reach were just star - fish on the

More Sing-Along Fun

LOVE LETTERS IN THE SAND

Verse 1
The sunbeams kissed the sands,
My fate was in your hands
The day I met you, dear.
And though I find you've gone,
Your mem'ry lingers on,
I can't forget you, dear.

Chorus
On a day like today,
We passed the time away
Writing Love Letters In The Sand.
How you laughed when I cried
Each time I saw the tide,
Take our Love Letters In The Sand.
You made a vow that you would always be true,
But somehow that vow meant nothing to you.
Now my poor heart just aches,
With ev'ry wave it breaks
Over Love Letters In The Sand.

Verse 2
While precious teardrops fall,
Your mem'ry I recall,
And days that used to be.
The skies were blue above,
It was the dawn of love,
But you've forgotten me.

Words by Nick and Charles Kenny   Music by J. Fred Coots
© Copyright 1931 by Bourne Co., New York, N.Y. Copyright renewed.

THEN I'LL BE HAPPY

I wanna go where you go,
Do what you do,
Love when you love,
Then I'll Be Happy.
I wanna sigh when you sigh,
Cry when you cry,
Smile when you smile,
Then I'll Be Happy.
If you go North or South,
If you go East or West,
I'll follow you, sweetheart,
And share your little love nest.
I wanna go where you go,
Do what you do,
Love when you love,
Then I'll Be Happy.

Words by Sidney Clare and Lew Brown   Music by Cliff Friend
© Copyright 1925 by Bourne Co., New York, N.Y. Copyright renewed.

CHARLEY, MY BOY

Verse 1
Charley is an ordinary fellow,
To most ev'ry one but Flo, his Flo.
She's convinced that Charley is a very
Extraordinary beau, some beau.
And ev'ry evening in the dim light,
She has a way of putting him right.

Chorus 1
Charley, My Boy, oh, Charley, My Boy,
You thrill me, you chill me, with shivers of joy.
You've got that kinda sorta bit of a way,
That makes me, takes me, tell me what shall I say.
And when we dance I read in your glance,
Whole pages and ages of love and romance.
They tell me Romeo was some lover too,
But boy, he should have taken lessons from you,
You seem to start where others get through,
Oh, Charley, My Boy.

Verse 2
Charley's Dad and Mother and his sister,
And his brother call him pest, just pest.
While his girl's relations say if he would
Stay away we'd have some rest, some rest.
Her father's cleaning up his rifle,
But she says dearie that's a trifle.

Chorus 2
Charley, My Boy, oh, Charley, My Boy,
You thrill me, you chill me, with shivers of joy.
You've got that kinda sorta bit of a way,
That makes me, takes me, tell me what shall I say,
And when we dance I read in your glance,
Sweet notions and oceans of love and romance.
My mother told me that I shouldn't be kissed,
But then your coaxing ways are hard to resist,
My lips refuse but your eyes insist,
Oh, Charley, My Boy.

Words and Music by Gus Kahn and Ted Fiorito
© Copyright 1924 by Bourne Co., New York, N.Y. Copyright renewed.

HEY, MR. BANJO

Hey, Mister Banjo, play a tune for me,
Play, Mister Banjo, a happy melody.
We'll all clap our hands,
And we'll stamp our feet,
You keep strummin' while we keep the beat,
Play, Mister Banjo, a pretty melody.

Hey, Mister Banjo, plunk another tune,
Hurry Mister Banjo, the night ends all too soon.
Make your banjo talk while we dance and sing,
Do a fancy walk while you pick those strings,
Hey, Mister Banjo, plunk a tune for me.

Hey, Mister Banjo, play us just one more,
Play, Mister Banjo, just like you did before.
When the stars are high, and the moon is low,
Keep a-strummin' on your old banjo,
Hey, Mister Banjo, play a tune for me.

Words and Music by Freddy Morgan and Norman Malkin

© Copyright 1955 by Mills Music, Inc.

GOODBYE, MY CONEY ISLAND BABY

Verse 1
We all fall for some girl that dresses neat,
Some girl that's got big feet,
We meet her on the street;
Then we'll join the army of married boobs,
To the altar, just like leading lambs to slaughter.

Chorus
Goodbye, My Coney Island Baby,
Farewell my own true love.
I'm gonna go away and leave you,
Never to see you anymore.
I'm goin' to sail upon that ferry boat,
Never to return again.
So goodbye, farewell, so long forever,
Goodbye, my Coney Isle, goodbye, my Coney Isle,
Goodbye, my Coney Island Babe.

Verse 2
When it's over, oh boy we get it good,
Bachelor days we then recall,
Rich man, poor man, beggar man, thief,
Doctor, lawyer, merchant chief,
We all are bound for matrimony.

Words and Music by Les Applegate

© Copyright 1948 by Mills Music, Inc.

IT'S ONLY A PAPER MOON

Verse
I never feel a thing is real, when I'm away from you,
Out of your embrace, the world's a temporary parking place.
Mmm, mm, mm, mm, a bubble for a minute,
Mm, mm, you smile, the bubble has a rainbow in it.

Chorus
Say, It's Only A Paper Moon, sailing over a cardboard sea,
But it wouldn't be make believe, if you believed in me.
Yes, it's only a canvas sky, hanging over a muslin tree,
But it wouldn't be make believe, if you believed in me.
Without your love, it's a honky-tonk parade,
Without your love, it's a melody played in a penny arcade.
It's a Barnum and Bailey world, just as phony as it can be,
But it wouldn't be make believe, if you believed in me.

Words by Billy Rose and E. Y. Harburg   Music by Harold Arlen

© Copyright 1933 by Harms, Inc. Copyright renewed.

BYE BYE BLUES

Verse
I got a big surprise, when I saw you smile
I never dreamed that it could be
But now I realize since I saw you smile,
There's only happiness for me. So . . .

Chorus
Bye Bye Blues, Bye Bye Blues,
Bells ring, birds sing,
Sun is shining, no more pining,
Just we two smiling thru,
Don't sigh, don't cry,
Bye Bye Blues.

Words and Music by Fred Hamm, Dave Bennett, Bert Lown, and Chauncey Gray

© Copyright 1930 by Bourne Co., New York, N.Y. Copyright renewed.

HOME

Verse
Ev'ning marks the close of day,
Skies of blue begin to grey,
Crimson hues are fading in the West;
Ev'ning ever brings to me
Dreams of days that used to be,
Memories of those I love the best.

Chorus
When shadows fall, and trees whisper day is ending,
My thoughts are ever wending Home.
When crickets call, my heart is forever yearning,
Once more to be returning Home.
When the hills conceal the setting sun,
Stars begin a-peeping one by one.
Night covers all, and, though fortune may forsake me,
Sweet dreams will ever take me Home.

Words and Music by Peter Van Steeden and Harry and Jeff Clarkson

© Copyright 1931 by Mills Music Inc. Copyright renewed 1959.

Songs from Movies

Movies and music were together long before the days of the "100%
All-Talking Pictures." Every movie house had its resident
piano player. And the very elegant ones even had orchestras.

Warner Brothers introduced "sound" in the mid-twenties with
something called Vitaphone. It was nothing more than a record
player hooked up to the projector, but it was a good gimmick. Al
Jolson's *The Jazz Singer*, made in 1927, was supposed to have
been just one of a series of Vitaphone films, with Jolson singing his
musical numbers and titles telling the audience what he was
saying when he spoke. But Jolson was always a great ad-libber, and
one day he talked to the orchestra when he was supposed
to be singing. The Warner Brothers, intrigued, left the ad-libbing on
the sound track. Audiences were spellbound—and talkies
were on their way in.

The Jazz Singer, a drama with music added, was soon followed by
the first screen musical, MGM's *Broadway Melody* (1929).
Gold Diggers of Broadway, another early musical film, featured "Tiptoe
Through The Tulips" in a spectacular production number.
Close-ups and cross-cutting here made the presentation of the song
far more impressive than it would have been on the stage.

After hearing of the talkies, Broadway musicians headed for
Hollywood in droves. Sometimes, they would turn their own
Broadway material into films. Cole Porter's *Gay Divorce*, for example,
became the Fred Astaire-Ginger Rogers *Gay Divorcee* in
1934. In other instances, musicians from Broadway would compose new
scores. Gershwin did for *A Damsel In Distress*, which
introduced "A Foggy Day."

Finally, there were composers and lyricists who made their name
in Hollywood. Henry Mancini, who scored *The Days Of
Wine And Roses*, and Max Steiner, who, in over 30 years in Hollywood,
has contributed to more than 100 films, including
Gone With The Wind, probably are the most famous of
Hollywood's stable of musical greats.

From those first scratchy experiments with sound to today's big-
sound stereo, the movie musical and the use of music in
movies have been an important part of America's musical heritage.
And it's been the movies and their worldwide charisma
that have introduced the songs of America to the rest of the world.

150

What makes a movie great? Story, acting, directing, photography, music? Whatever
standards are used to judge motion picture achievement, you come out
with one all-time film classic—*Gone With The Wind*.

This 1939 film, based on Margaret Mitchell's epic novel, has broken all box
office records and continues to excite generation after generation of
movie-goers. The writer of the movie score, Max Steiner, was a specialist in the
field. His music scores underlined many of the MGM hits of the period.

The hauntingly beautiful "Tara's Theme" was the instrumental background in
the movie. Its title came from the name of Scarlett O'Hara's home. This
poignant melody captured the film's mood and the bittersweet life of Scarlett.

While "Tara's Theme" received its share of accolades and became a popular
instrumental number, it wasn't until 1954 that lyrics were added. The
new rendition "My Own True Love," started a brand-new whirlwind of enthusiasm.

Writer Mack David was responsible for the lyrics, and the combination
of David and Steiner proves that even what's great often can be made greater. Now,
lovers of Steiner's time-honored melody can add another dimension to
their appreciation with David's lyrics. The result is a song that, in its own right,
is the same kind of classic as *Gone With The Wind*.

MY OWN TRUE LOVE

based on TARA THEME from the motion picture
"GONE WITH THE WIND"

Words by
MACK DAVID

Music by
MAX STEINER

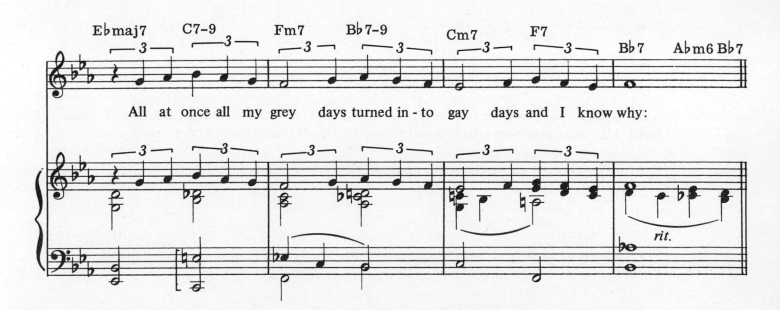

Chorus:

My Own True Love, My Own True Love,

At last I've found you, My Own True Love,

No lips but yours, No arms but yours Will ev - er

lead me through heav - en's doors; I roamed the earth

In search of this,   I knew I'd know you,

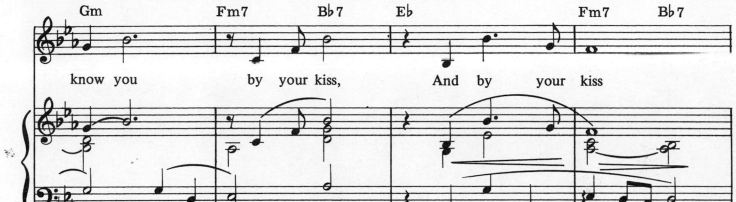

know you   by your kiss,   And by your kiss

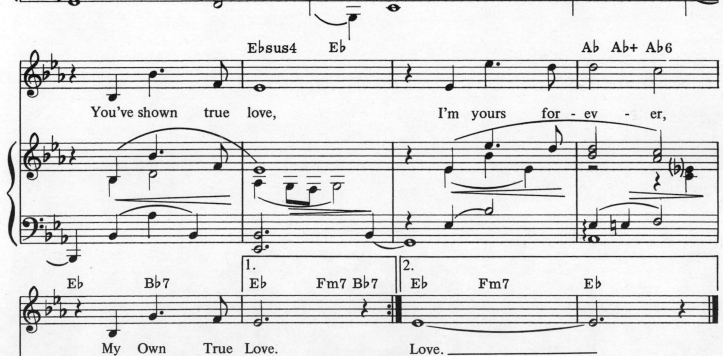

You've shown true love,   I'm yours for - ev - er,

My Own True Love.   Love.

Whistle While You Work

There probably are not too many Americans over the age of ten who have not sat in a movie theater, clutching popcorn and sighing over the beauty of Snow White—gasping with fear as she ate the poisoned apple—or chuckled with the Seven Dwarfs as they trudged off to work.

Snow White And The Seven Dwarfs is truly a film classic. It was the first full-length animated motion picture and has, since its premiere in 1937, withstood the ravages of time, critics, and audience cynicism.

The film's creator, the late Walt Disney, is recognized as a creative genius in the field of animation, but few give him credit for his knowledge of how important the blend of audio and visual is. His use of music in the animated films he created is superb, and *Snow White And The Seven Dwarfs* is one of his finest examples. Starting with the love song, "Someday My Prince Will Come," straight through to the dwarfs' big number, "Whistle While You Work," the music is a perfect setting for these animated characters.

Songwriters Larry Morey and Frank Churchill created this music, which did much more than convey a vocal message. It projected personalities as well. The music expressed the sweet innocence of Snow White and showcased all the impish humor of the Seven Dwarfs.

"Whistle While You Work" is a happy song sung by happy people. It may be a far cry from the work songs of American railroaders or miners, but the Dwarfs were not like any other workers—before or since. They were unique in their inception, animation, and music. Long live their uniqueness.

WHISTLE WHILE YOU WORK

Words by
LARRY MOREY

Music by
FRANK CHURCHILL

Verse:

When the work be - gins to pile up, And your tem - per starts to rile up,

That's the time a fel - low needs a song.

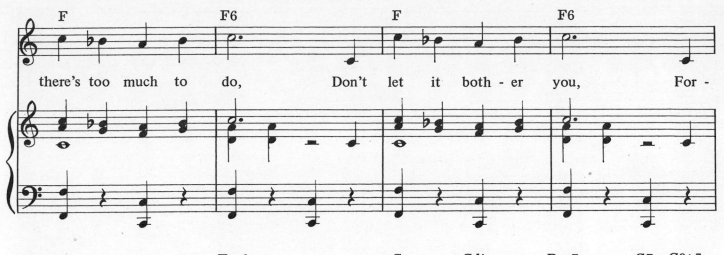

there's too much to do, Don't let it both - er you, For -

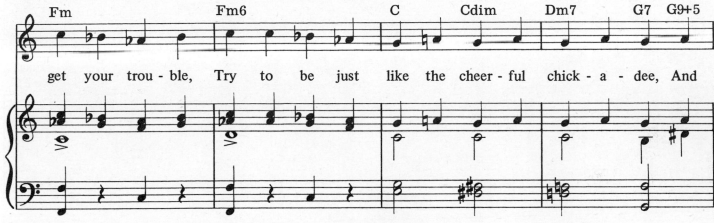

get your trou - ble, Try to be just like the cheer - ful chick - a - dee, And

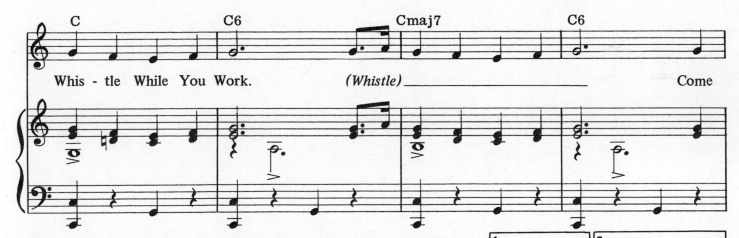

Whis - tle While You Work. *(Whistle)* _____ Come

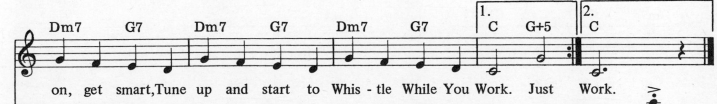

on, get smart, Tune up and start to Whis - tle While You Work. Just Work.

Days of Wine and Roses

Music by HENRY MANCINI

Words by JOHNNY MERCER

Jack Lemmon and Lee Remick

in "Days of Wine and Roses"

CHARLES **BICKFORD** JACK **KLUGMAN** **A MARTIN MANULIS Production** Music by **HENRY MANCINI** Written by **JP MILLER** Produced by **MARTIN MANULIS** Directed by **BLAKE EDWARDS** Presented by **WARNER BROS.**

Price **60¢** in U.S.A.

M. WITMARK & SONS • NEW YORK, NEW YORK

Printed in U.S.A.

Henry Mancini

Days of Wine and Roses

Creating movie music is "a very delicate craft" according to Henry Mancini—and who should know more about the craft than a man who has composed scores for several of the most important films made since the early '60s? Henry Mancini's portfolio of best-selling songs is comparable to that of any composer of any era—one of the most beautiful songs is his theme from the movie *Days Of Wine And Roses.*

This song, like most of the other Mancini hits, was created to augment the film, not as a single singable melody. Mancini has been quoted as saying, "I want to do my job for the picture honestly. I always approach a score as to what is best for the picture—not what's best for a record album, or the shortest cut to a hit song." But strangely enough, every movie score composed by Mancini seems to produce not one, but usually several separate songs—many of them on their way to being hits after the movie is released.

"Days Of Wine And Roses" won an Oscar for Henry Mancini and lyricist Johnny Mercer in 1962, just one year after the same coveted award had been presented to the songwriting team for "Moon River." This was a Hollywood first. No songwriting team had every won back-to-back Oscars—nor has any since. But those are the kind of successes that can be expected from this inventive composer.

Mancini's hit songs are only one aspect of his far-reaching contribution to movie music. The general quality of his entire score is noteworthy, too. Each of the scores is stocked with melodic motifs that could very well acquire lyrics someday and be revived as separate songs. If someone does accept this challenge, we can expect more hits that carry the credit, "Music by Henry Mancini."

DAYS OF WINE AND ROSES

Lyric by
JOHNNY MERCER

Music by
HENRY MANCINI

The Days Of Wine And Ros - es

Laugh and run a - way Like a child at play, Through the

mead - ow - land to - ward a clos - ing door, A door marked "Nev - er - more," That

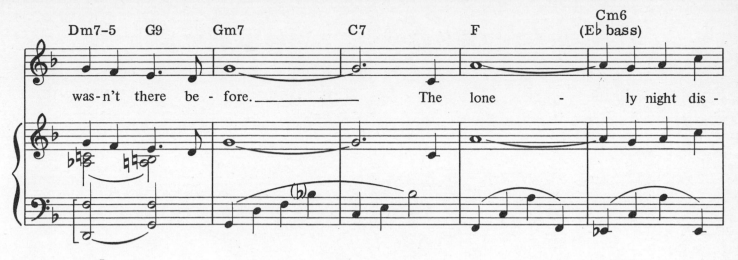

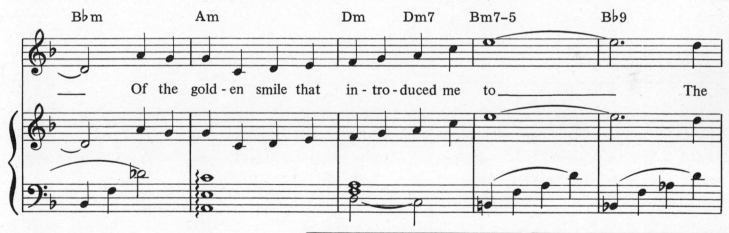

The movie was *Casablanca;* the scene, a nightclub in that North African town; the star, Humphrey Bogart playing Rick Blaine, nightclub owner. "Play it again, Sam," he says to the pianist in that dead-pan voice of his. Dooley Wilson knows what he means and strikes into Herman Hupfeld's 1931 "As Time Goes By," which debuted in the musical *Everybody's Welcome*. Although Rudy Vallee recorded the song originally, it wasn't too successful until the 1942 *Casablanca*, in which it took on a certain something from the association with Bogart, Ingrid Bergman, and a sad love story.

By the time you hear "As Time Goes By" in the film, you know what it means to Rick. With it, he had once wooed Ilsa Lund (played by Ingrid Bergman). She was a widow—or so they both thought. When she finds out differently, she can't tell Rick. And when he finds out accidentally, Rick thinks he's been jilted and nurses his bitterness through wanderings that finally land him in Casablanca, a stop on the escape route from war-torn Europe.

Then one day, Ilsa, fleeing Europe with her husband, walks into his cafe. They're still in love, but it's emotion against duty. Rick takes the noble course and comes out looking so good that years later Woody Allen would use Bogart to symbolize masculine strength in *Play It Again, Sam*.

AS TIME GOES BY

Words and Music by
HERMAN HUPFELD

Verse:

This day and age we're liv-ing in gives cause for ap-pre-hen-sion, With

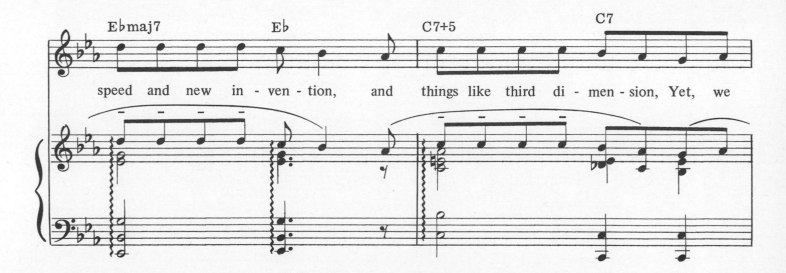

speed and new in-ven-tion, and things like third di-men-sion, Yet, we

get a tri - fle wea - ry with Mis - ter Ein - stein's the - 'ry, So we

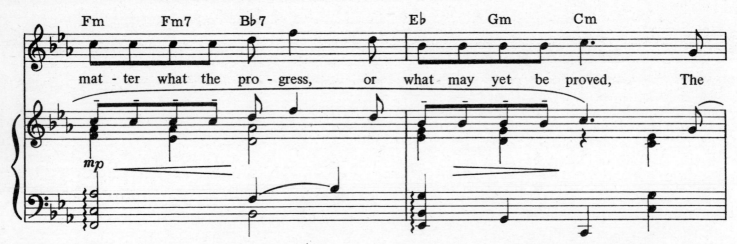

must get down to earth, at times re - lax, re - lieve the ten - sion. No

mat - ter what the pro - gress, or what may yet be proved, The

sim - ple facts of life are such they can - not be re - moved.

Chorus:

You must re-mem - ber this, a kiss is still a kiss, A

sigh is just a sigh; The fun - da - men - tal things ap -

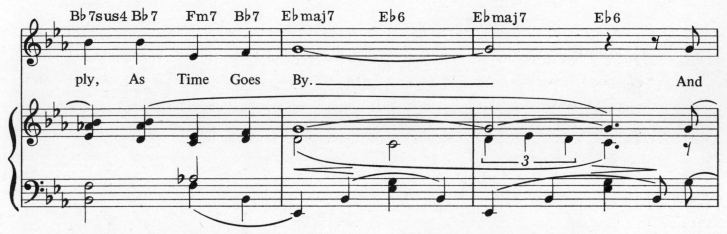

ply, As Time Goes By. _____ And

when two lov - ers woo, they still say, "I love you," On

no one can de - ny. It's still the same old sto - ry, a

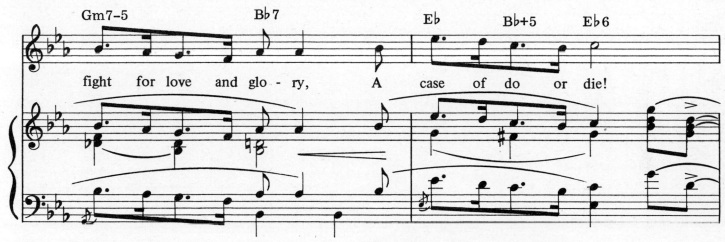

fight for love and glo - ry, A case of do or die!

The world will al - ways wel - come lov - ers, As

Time Goes By. You By.

Other Hits From Movies

IT'S MAGIC

Verse
I've heard about Houdini and the rest of them,
And I'd put you up against the best of them,
As far as I'm concerned, you're the tops, and you don't resort to props;
Things I used to think were inconceivable,
You've a way of making them believable,
And upon a night like this I'm afraid you just can't miss.

Chorus
You sigh, the song begins, you speak and I hear violins, It's Magic.
The stars desert the skies and rush to nestle in your eyes, It's Magic.
Without a golden wand or mystic charms
Fantastic things begin when I am in your arms.
When we walk hand in hand, the world becomes a wonderland, It's Magic.
How else can I explain those rainbows when there is no rain, It's Magic.
Why do I tell myself these things that happen are all really true,
When in my heart I know the magic is my love for you.

Words by Sammy Cahn   Music by Jule Styne

© Copyright 1948 by M. Witmark & Sons

GIGI

Verse
There's sweeter music when she speaks, isn't there?
A diff'rent bloom about her cheeks, isn't there?
Could I be wrong? Could it be so?
Oh where, oh where did Gigi go?

Chorus
Gigi, am I a fool without a mind
Or have I merely been too blind to realize?
Oh Gigi, why you've been growing up before my eyes!
Gigi, you're not at all that funny, awkward little girl I knew.
Oh no! Over night there's been a breathless change in you.

Oh, Gigi, while you were trembling on the brink,
Was I out yonder somewhere blinking at a star?
Oh, Gigi, have I been standing up too close, or back too far?
When did your sparkle turn to fire and your warmth become desire?
Oh, what miracle has made you the way you are?

Gigi, am I a fool without a mind
Or have I merely been too blind to realize?
Oh, Gigi, why you've been growing up before my eyes!
Gigi, you're not at all that funny, awkward little girl I knew,
Oh no! I was mad not to have seen the change in you!

Oh, Gigi, while you were trembling on the brink,
Was I out yonder somewhere blinking at a star?
Oh Gigi, have I been standing up too close, or back too far?
When did your sparkle turn to fire and your warmth become desire?
Oh, what miracle has made you the way you are?

Words by Alan Jay Lerner   Music by Frederick Loewe

Copyright © 1957 (unpub) & 1958 by Chappell & Co., Inc.

I ENJOY BEING A GIRL

Verse
I'm a girl, and by me that's only great!
I am proud that my silhouette is curvy,
That I walk with a sweet and girlish gait
With my hips kind of swively and swervy,
I adore being dressed in something frilly
When my date comes to get me at my place.
Out I go with my Joe or John or Billy,
Like a filly who is ready for the race!

Chorus
When I have a brand new hairdo
With my eyelashes all in curl,
I float as the clouds on air do,
I Enjoy Being A Girl!
When men say I'm cute and funny
And my teeth aren't teeth but pearl,
I just lap it up like honey,
I Enjoy Being A Girl!
I flip when a fellow sends me flowers,
I drool over dresses made of lace,
I talk on the telephone for hours
With a pound and a half of cream upon my face!
I'm strictly a female female
And my future I hope will be
In the home of a brave and free male
Who'll enjoy being a guy having a girl like me.

Words by Oscar Hammerstein II   Music by Richard Rodgers

Copyright © 1958 by Richard Rodgers & Oscar Hammerstein II

Williamson Music, Inc., owner of publication and allied rights
for the Western Hemisphere & Japan.

STORMY WEATHER

Don't know why there's no sun up in the sky,
Stormy Weather,
Since my man and I ain't together,
Keeps rainin' all the time.

Life is bare, gloom and mis'ry everywhere,
Stormy Weather,
Just can't get my poor self together,
I'm weary all the time, the time,
So weary all the time.

When he went away, the blues walked in and met me,
If he stays away, old rockin' chair will get me.
All I do is pray the Lord above will let me
Walk in the sun once more.

Can't go on, everything I had is gone,
Stormy Weather,
Since my man and I ain't together,
Keeps rainin' all the time,
Keeps rainin' all the time.

Words by Ted Koehler   Music by Harold Arlen

© Copyright 1933 by Mills Music. Copyright renewed 1961 by Arko Music Corp.

EXACTLY LIKE YOU

Verse
I used to have a perfect sweetheart,
Not a real one, just a dream,
A wonderful vision of us as a team,
Can you imagine how I feel now,
Love is real, it's ideal
You're just what I wanted,
And now it's nice to live,
Paradise to live:

Chorus
I know why I've waited,
Know why I've been blue,
Prayed each night for someone
Exactly Like You.
Why should we spend money
On a show or two,
No one does those love scenes
Exactly Like You.
You make me feel so grand,
I want to hand the world to you,
You seem to understand
Each foolish little scheme I'm scheming,
Dream I'm dreaming.
Now I know why mother
Taught me to be true.
She meant me for someone
Exactly Like You.

Words by Dorothy Fields   Music by Jimmy McHugh
© Copyright 1930 by Shapiro, Bernstein & Co. Copyright renewed.

DON'T FENCE ME IN

Verse
Wild Cat Kelly, looking mighty pale,
Was standing by the sheriff's side.
And when that sheriff said, "I'm sending you to jail,"
Wild Cat raised his head and cried:

Chorus
Oh, give me land, lots of land under starry skies above
Don't Fence Me In,
Let me ride thru the wide open country that I love,
Don't Fence Me In.
Let me be by myself in the evening breeze
Listen to the murmur of the cottonwood trees.
Send me off forever, but I ask you please
Don't Fence Me In.
Just turn me loose,
Let me straddle my old saddle underneath the western skies.
On my cayuse,
Let me wander over yonder till I see the mountains rise.
I want to ride to the ridge where the West commences,
Gaze at the moon till I lose my senses,
Can't look at hobbles and I can't stand fences,
Don't Fence Me In.

Words and Music by Cole Porter
© Copyright 1944 by Harms, Inc. Copyright renewed.

MY FAVORITE THINGS

Raindrops on roses and whiskers on kittens,
Bright copper kettles and warm woolen mittens,
Brown paper packages tied up with strings,
These are a few of My Favorite Things.

Cream colored ponies and crisp apple strudels,
Doorbells and sleigh bells and schnitzel with noodles,
Wild geese that fly with the moon on their wings,
These are a few of My Favorite Things.

Girls in white dresses and blue satin sashes,
Snowflakes that stay on my nose and eyelashes,
Silver white winters that melt into springs,
These are a few of My Favorite Things.

When the dog bites,
When the bee stings,
When I'm feeling sad,
I simply remember My Favorite Things
And then I don't feel so bad.

Words by Oscar Hammerstein II   Music by Richard Rodgers
Copyright © 1959 by Richard Rodgers and Oscar Hammerstein II
Williamson Music, Inc., owner of publication and allied rights
for the Western Hemisphere & Japan.

BLUES IN THE NIGHT

My mama done tol' me
When I was in kneepants,
My mama done tol' me, Son!
A woman 'll sweet talk
And give ya the big eye,
But when the sweet talkin's done,
A woman's a two-face,
A worrisome thing who'll leave ya t' sing
The Blues In The Night.
Now the rain's a-fallin'
Hear the train a-callin', whooee,
(My mama done tol' me.)
Hear dat lonesome whistle
Blowin' 'cross the trestle, whooee,
(My mama done tol' me,)
A whooee duh whooee,
Ol' clickety clack's a-echoin' back
Th' Blues In The Night.
The evenin' breeze 'll start the trees
To cryin' and the moon 'll hide its light,
When you get the Blues In The Night.
Take my word, the mockin' bird 'll
Sing the saddest kind o' song,
He knows things are wrong and he's right.
From Natchez to Mobile,
From Memphis to St. Joe,
Wherever the four winds blow;
I been in some big towns
An' heard me some big talk,
But there is one thing I know,
A woman's a two-face,
A worrisome thing who'll leave ya t' sing
The Blues In The Night.
My mama was right,
There's Blues In The Night.

Words by Johnny Mercer   Music by Harold Arlen
© Copyright 1941 by Remick Music Corp. Copyright renewed.

Songs from Plays

Ever since minstrel Dan Emmett wrote "Dixie's Land" in the mid-nineteenth century, the American theater has spawned some of this country's best songs. And nearly every important star in show business has at one time or other displayed his talent "on the boards." Had it not been for a man named Tony Pastor, though, respectable people may never have had the chance to enjoy the songs or the entertainers.

Back then, ladies didn't go to the theater. Oh, they knew all about it—the men smoked, drank, and cursed, and the women on stage showed their legs. Tony Pastor, who saw women and children as a vast, untapped audience, started presenting "wholesome entertainments" in 1865, first in New Jersey, then in New York, where he started a whole new era in the theater with a stroke of genius—door prizes. He offered the women half-barrels of flour, dress patterns, kitchenware, and coal, and they came in droves. Eventually, even the stuffiest families were enjoying vaudeville hits.

On Broadway, vaudeville gave way in the teens to the revue—a sequined and satin-clad expansion of the vaudeville show—in which one composer-lyricist team wrote all the music. George Gershwin, who went on to write America's first folk opera, and Irving Berlin both wrote for Florenz Ziegfeld's *Follies* and George White's *Scandals*.

In the thirties, at about the time Jimmy McHugh and Dorothy Fields wrote "On The Sunny Side Of The Street" for the *International Revue*, musical comedy, which is regarded as America's most important contribution to the theater, was taking over Broadway stages and bringing new composers and songs to the theaters.

George M. Cohan presented the first musical, *Little Johnny Jones*, which introduced "Yankee Doodle Dandy" and "Give My Regards To Broadway." That was in 1904, and critics called Cohan's work lively but uncouth and certainly naive. Musicals really took off with the work of Jerome Kern, George Gershwin, Irving Berlin, and Richard Rodgers, first working with Lorenz Hart and later with Oscar Hammerstein II. And Alan Lerner and Frederick Loewe brought back some of the theater's lost elegance in *My Fair Lady*, which added songs such as "I Could Have Danced All Night" and "On The Street Where You Live" to a long list of wonderful music.

Give My Regards to Broadway

Although just 26 years old when he wrote "Give My Regards To Broadway," George M. Cohan already had logged
nearly a quarter-century around the theater with his actor-parents. And when the song debuted in the 1904 musical *Little
Johnny Jones*, it expressed Cohan's high hopes for success on Broadway. As for *Little Johnny Jones*, the critics
found its exuberance crude and naive. Despite bad reviews, Cohan was not daunted. He packed up the show and took it on
the road—and audiences loved it. When a polished-up production returned to New York, it caught on and so did
George M. Cohan. Soon, he had the power to push performers to stardom; soon, he was rich enough to pay their rent, if need be.

Those happy years ran out all too quickly, though.
Not all producers were as generous as Cohan, and actors unionized and called a strike that closed down 24 shows.
When Cohan saw many of the people he'd helped out on the other side of the picket lines, he felt that Broadway
had betrayed him. He did everything he could to fight this new Actors Equity Association—and kept on fighting with
a bitterness that finally took the fun out of the theater for him.

Broadway was changing, too. The confident America
of the teens of which Cohan had been so much a part had entered a bewildering era. Audiences wanted the theater to
help them sort things out, and here was Cohan giving them simple superpatriotic entertainments. Cohan
productions after 1920 rarely took hold. His Broadway love song of 1904 was bittersweet; the affair was over, and
Cohan's exuberance had gone with it. "They don't want me no more," he said, and in 1940, the "founding father" of Broadway
musical comedy left the Great White Way forever.

GIVE MY REGARDS TO BROADWAY

Words and Music by
GEORGE M. COHAN

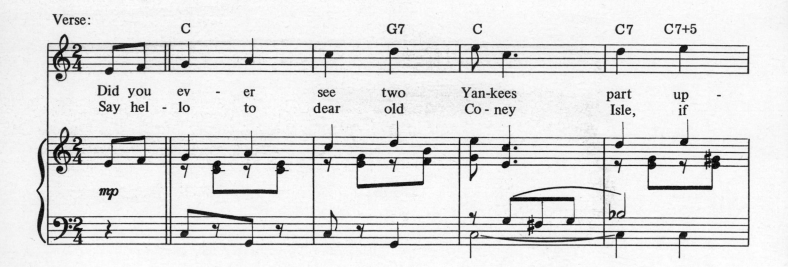

Did you ev - er see two Yan-kees part up -
Say hel - lo to dear old Co - ney Isle, if

on a for - eign shore,_____ When the good ship's
there you chance to be;_____ When you're at the

On the Sunny Side of the Street

By 1930 the revue, which once had been the backbone of Broadway, had almost run its course. So, it's not surprising that when Lew Leslie staged his *International Revue*, it flopped—the production closed down after only 95 performances. The only successful thing about the revue was the Jimmy McHugh-Dorothy Fields song "On The Sunny Side Of The Street."

Revues had started out in 1894 as a more elaborate form of vaudeville show. And unlike their earlier counterparts, in revues, material was written expressly for the production rather than supplied by the individual performers. Spectacles such as Ziegfeld's *Follies*, George White's *Scandals*, the Shuberts' *Passing Shows*, and Earl Carroll's *Vanities* were a proving ground for thousands of songs and for nearly every important creative or performing talent in America. And with stars descending black velvet staircases, coming on stage on trapezes and springing out of trap doors, and wearing gowns dripping with silver sequins, revues were sheer delight for costumers and set designers.

With the advent of the Depression, though, theatergoers were looking for more substantial entertainment. The few revues that did make it in the late twenties and thirties, such as *As Thousands Cheer*, did so as social commentaries.

"On The Sunny Side Of The Street" had the long career it deserved off-Broadway. It was the title for a 1951 Columbia Pictures movie and was used in the Ted Lewis biography *Is Everybody Happy?*, the musical *Two Blondes And A Redhead*, *The Eddy Duchin Story*, *The Benny Goodman Story*, and *The Helen Morgan Story*. And, it has been recorded by Bing Crosby, Jo Stafford, Benny Goodman, Ted Lewis, Tommy Dorsey, Earl Hines, Judy Garland, and many others.

ON THE SUNNY SIDE OF THE STREET

Lyric by
DOROTHY FIELDS

Music by
JIMMY McHUGH

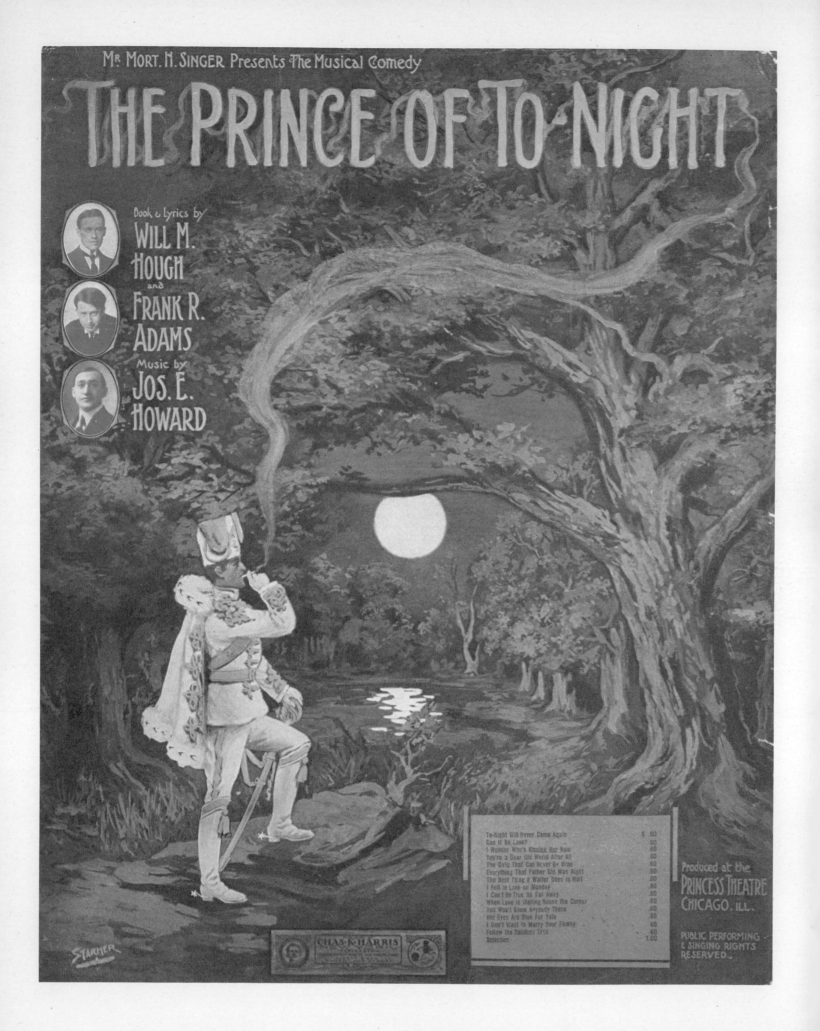

I Wonder Who's Kissing Her Now

America was starved for entertainment as the calendar
turned over a new century, and appetites were appeased by
spectacular circuses, silent movies, and legitimate
theater. Stage plays generated enthusiasm that set new records.

With Broadway booming and Tin Pan Alley publishing
music for a waiting nation, it's no wonder that a good many of
the stage offerings in the early 1900s were musicals or revues.

One of the 1909 Broadway openings was a production
titled *The Prince Of Tonight,* a combined effort of musical/comedy
writer Joe Howard and the team of Will M. Hough and
Frank R. Adams. The show seems to have faded into obscurity,
but one of its songs will be remembered forever.
"I Wonder Who's Kissing Her Now" gained immediate success.

The song also appeared in the screen version of
another Howard musical comedy, *The Time, The Place, And The
Girl.* And for years, starting in 1909, Howard
would sing "I Wonder Who's Kissing Her Now" every time he
made a public appearance—for almost half a century.

Though this was considered Joe Howard's best-known song,
the strange fact is that Howard did not write it. This
came to light in 1947 when Hollywood got around to filming his
screen biography, *I Wonder Who's Kissing Her Now.*
Shortly after the movie's release, a man named Harold Orlob
stepped forward to claim the authorship of the song.
He had worked for Howard in 1909 and writing the song had been
part of the job. Howard, of course, had viewed the
song as his property and palmed it off as his own—and indeed,
that was the usual practice back then. Orlob was
asking for no damages. He just wanted his name on the piece.
The settlement, made out of court, made Orlob co-author.

I WONDER WHO'S KISSING HER NOW

Lyric by
HOUGH & ADAMS
French Lyric by
PAUL PIERROT

Music by
JOSEPH E. HOWARD
and **HAROLD ORLOB**

Moderately

Verse:

You have loved lots of girls in the sweet long a - go, And each
If you want to feel wretch - ed and lone - ly and blue, Just im -
Beau - coup d'a - mours vous a - vez eu dans le pas - sé, Et cha -

one has meant heav - en to you, _____ You have vowed your af -
ag - ine the girl you love best _____ In the arms of some
cun tom - bait du ciel pour vous; _____ En re - tour vous fai -

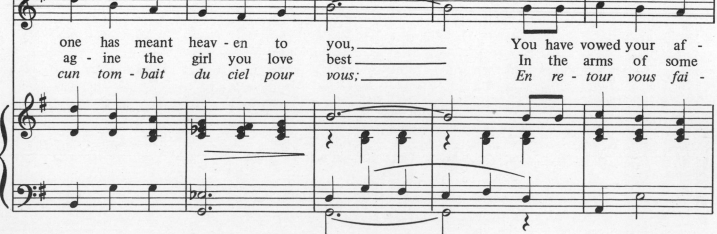

Most musicals include at least one straight-from-the-heart love song involving the male and female leads. Without it, an audience would probably feel cheated. Lerner and Loewe were all too aware of this fact when they created the music for *My Fair Lady*. And yet, the Bernard Shaw play, *Pygmalion*, from which the musical was adapted, carefully excluded any affirmation of love. So the composers' challenge was to create a song that the audience would accept as a love song, but that would not suggest a developing attachment between Professor Higgins and his pupil Eliza Doolittle. After months of work, the song that emerged was "I Could Have Danced All Night."

This exhilarating number is performed after Eliza's first successful pronunciation session, when Higgins, in his excitement, drops his guard long enough to lead her through a tango. Later, after the Professor (Rex Harrison) has left the study, Eliza continues to dance. Julie Andrews charmed audiences with her portrayal of Eliza, whirling and turning and expressing her satisfaction with herself and her attachment for Higgins.

"I Could Have Danced All Night" needed to be a song that conveyed a subtle bit of stage business, yet one that gave the audience what it expected—a love song. On both counts, the Lerner and Loewe composition measures up.

I COULD HAVE DANCED ALL NIGHT

Words by
ALAN JAY LERNER

Music by
FREDERICK LOEWE

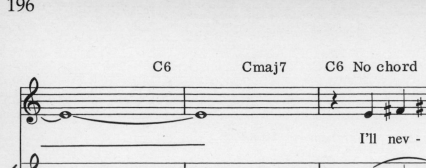

I'll nev-er know_____ what made it

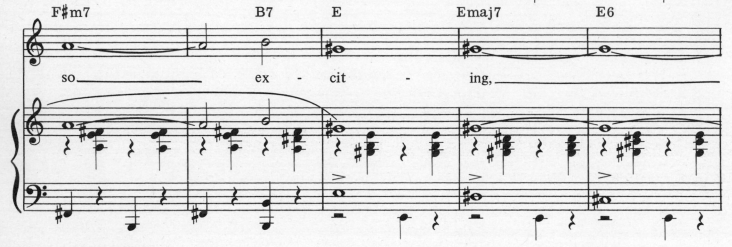

so_____ ex - cit - ing,_____

____ Why all at once_____ my heart took

flight._____ I on - ly know_____

SUMMERTIME

Lyrics by DuBOSE HEYWARD   Music by GEORGE GERSHWIN

SAMUEL GOLDWYN
presents
PORGY and BESS

starring
SIDNEY POITIER · DOROTHY DANDRIDGE
SAMMY DAVIS, Jr. · PEARL BAILEY
Music by GEORGE GERSHWIN · Libretto by DuBOSE HEYWARD
Lyrics by DuBOSE HEYWARD and IRA GERSHWIN
(Founded on the play 'Porgy' by DuBOSE and DOROTHY HEYWARD)
Originally produced for the stage by the Theatre Guild · Screenplay by N. RICHARD NASH

Also Published from the Score
SUMMERTIME
IT AIN'T NECESSARILY SO
BESS YOU IS MY WOMAN
I GOT PLENTY O' NUTTIN'
A WOMAN IS A SOMETIME THING

$1.00

Directed by OTTO PREMINGER · Distributed by COLUMBIA PICTURES
Produced In TODD-AO® · TECHNICOLOR®
STEREOPHONIC SOUND

5565023-101B

GERSHWIN PUBLISHING CORPORATION & CHAPPELL & CO., INC.   Sole Selling Agent, CHAPPELL & CO., INC.

Summertime

George Gershwin's enthusiasm for writing *Porgy And Bess*
began one evening in 1926 when he picked up
DuBose Heyward's novel *Porgy*, hoping to read himself to
sleep. The more he read, the more excited he became
about the book's possibilities, and at 4:00 a.m. he wrote the
author, detailing his idea.

Years went by, however, and work was never begun. Then,
in 1935, the Theater Guild contacted Heyward
with the idea of turning his story into a Jerome Kern musical
comedy starring Al Jolson. Gershwin asked Heyward
to hold off on the project until he could fulfill his other
commitments. Heyward did, and shortly thereafter,
production began.

The opening lullaby, "Summertime," is one of the most
beautiful and popular songs from the entire score. And
its soothing strains are a musical contrast to what audiences
see on the stage while the song is performed. The
setting is Catfish Row, a Negro tenement in Charleston, South
Carolina, and the action includes a crap game in
one corner of the court, while several other inhabitants
of the "row" are dancing amid the squalor. The
beauty of "Summertime" transcends a wretched environment.

In that same way, the opera *Porgy And Bess* transcended
the bad reviews of New York critics following its 1935 opening.
The critics reversed their opinions after the opera's
revival in 1942, when they labeled the work "a beautiful piece of
music and a deeply moving play for the lyric theater."

Porgy And Bess was Gershwin's last and most monumental
stage production. It took him nearly two years to write
and orchestrate the opera—some of this time was spent in South
Carolina learning the life and folk music of blacks.
The result: a folk opera that has become an epic of the black race.

SUMMERTIME

Lyrics by
DuBOSE HEYWARD

Music by
GEORGE GERSHWIN

Allegretto semplice

Moderato *(with expression)*

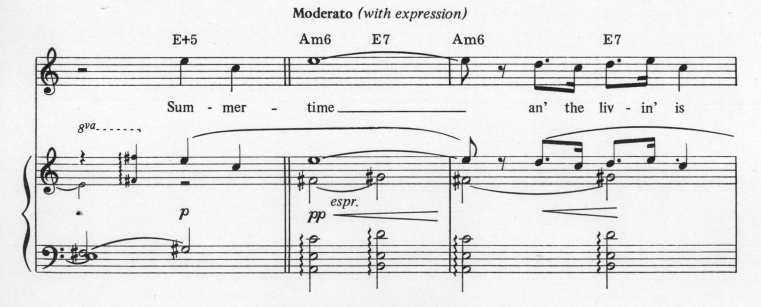

Sum - mer - time _____ an' the liv - in' is

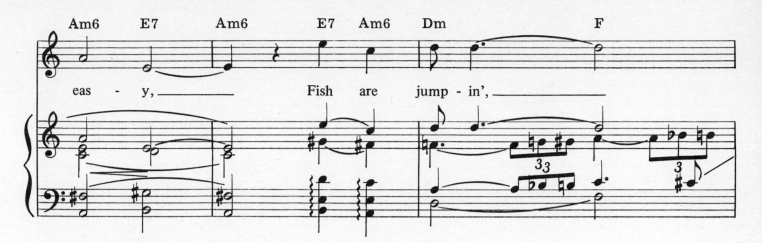

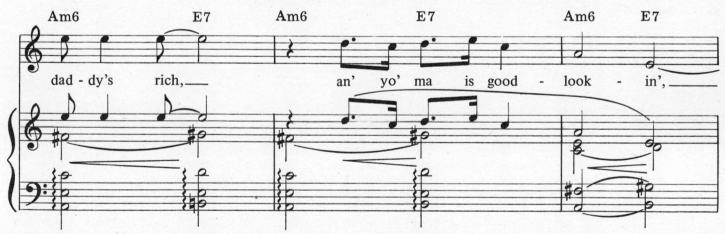

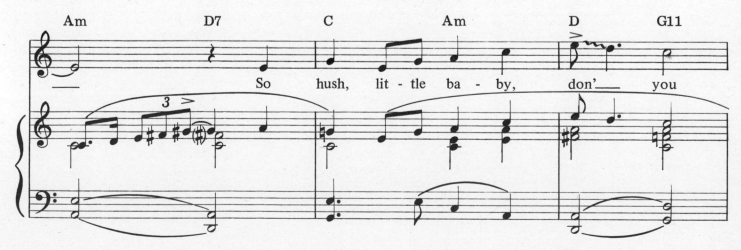

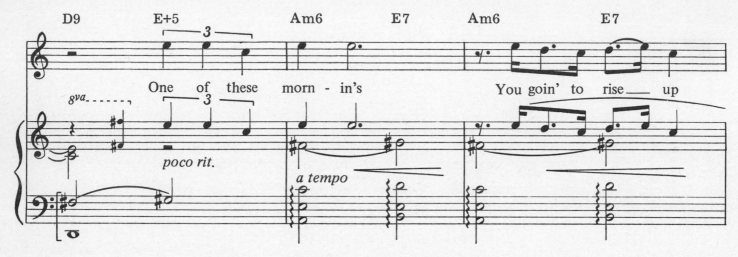

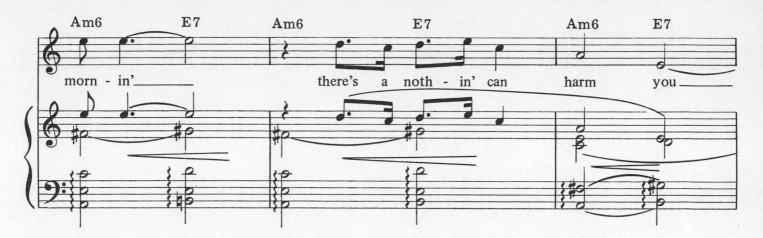

morn - in'_____ there's a noth - in' can harm you_____

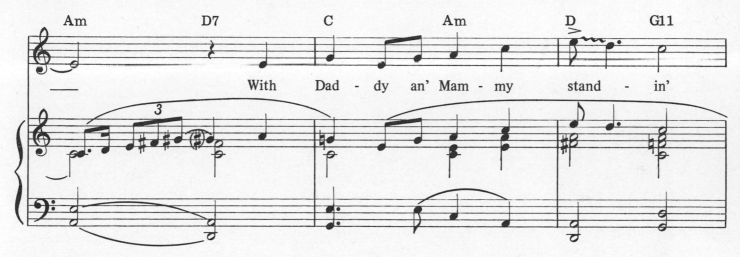

With Dad - dy an' Mam - my stand - in'

by. _____

More Broadway Show Hits

THESE FOOLISH THINGS

A cigarette that bears a lipstick's traces,
An airline ticket to romantic places,
And still my heart has wings.
These Foolish Things remind me of you.
A tinkling piano in the next apartment,
Those stumbling words that told you what my heart meant,
A fairground's painted swings,
These Foolish Things remind me of you.
You came, you saw, you conquer'd me;
When you did that to me,
I knew somehow this had to be.
The winds of March that make my heart a dancer,
A telephone that rings but who's to answer?
Oh, how the ghost of you clings!
These Foolish Things remind me of you.

Words by Holt Marvell   Music by Jack Strachey and Harry Link

© Copyright 1935 by Boosey & Hawkes, Ltd., England

Rights for United States, Canada, Newfoundland
assigned to Bourne Co., New York, N.Y. Copyright renewed.

YOU'RE THE CREAM IN MY COFFEE

Verse
I'm not a poet, how well I know it,
I've never been a raver, but when I speak of you
I rave a bit, it's true.
I'm wild about you, I'm lost without you,
You give my life its flavor,
What sugar does for tea, that's what you do for me.

Chorus
You're The Cream In My Coffee, you're the salt in my stew.
You will always be my necessity, I'd be lost without you.
You're the starch in my collar, you're the lace in my shoe,
You will always be my necessity, I'd be lost without you.
Most men tell lovetales, and each phrase dovetails,
You've heard each known way, this way is my own way.
You're the sail of my loveboat, you're the captain and crew,
You will always be my necessity, I'd be lost without you.

Words and Music by B. G. DeSylva, Lew Brown, and Ray Henderson

Copyright © 1928 by DeSylva, Brown & Henderson

Copyright renewed, assigned to Chappell & Co., Inc.

Published in the United States by joint agreement
with Chappell & Co., Inc. and Anne-Rachel Music Corporation.

THE BLUE ROOM

Verse
All my future plans, dear, will suit your plans,
Read the little blue prints;
Here's your mother's room, here's your brother's room,
On the wall are two prints.
Here's the kiddies' room, here's the biddy's room,
Here's a pantry lined with shelves, dear,
Here I've planned for us, something grand for us,
Where we two can be ourselves, dear.

Chorus
We'll have a blue room, a new room, for two room,
Where ev'ry day's a holiday because you're married to me.
Not like a ballroom, a small room, a hall room,
Where I can smoke my pipe away, with your wee head upon my knee.
We will thrive on, keep alive on just nothing but kisses,
With Mister and Missus on little blue chairs.
You sew your trousseau, and Robinson Crusoe
Is not so far from worldly cares as our blue room far away upstairs!

Words by Lorenz Hart   Music by Richard Rodgers

© Copyright 1926 by Harms, Inc. Copyright renewed 1959.

SOMEONE TO WATCH OVER ME

Verse
There's a saying old, says that love is blind,
Still we're often told, "Seek an ye shall find."
So I'm going to seek a certain lad I've had in mind.
Looking ev'rywhere, haven't found him yet;
He's the big affair I cannot forget.
Only man I ever think of with regret.
I'd like to add his initial to my monogram.
Tell me, where is the shepherd for this lost lamb.

Chorus
There's a somebody I'm longing to see,
I hope that he turns out to be
Someone who'll watch over me.
I'm a little lamb who's lost in the wood,
I know I could always be good
To one who'll watch over me.
Although he may not be the man some girls think of as handsome,
To my heart he carries the key.
Won't you tell him please to put on some speed,
Follow my lead, oh, how I need
Someone To Watch Over Me.

Words by Ira Gershwin   Music by George Gershwin

© Copyright 1926 by New World Music Corp. Copyright renewed 1950.

LIFE IS JUST A BOWL OF CHERRIES

Verse
People are queer, they're always crowing, scrambling and rushing about.
Why don't they stop some day, address themselves this way:
Why are we here? Where are we going? It's time that we found out
We're not here to stay, we're on a short holiday.

Chorus
Life Is Just A Bowl Of Cherries,
Don't make it serious, life's too mysterious.
You work, you save, you worry so,
But you can't take your dough when you go, go, go.
So keep repeating it's the berries,
The strongest oak must fall.
The sweet things in life to you were just loaned,
So how can you lose what you've never owned.
Life Is Just A Bowl Of Cherries,
So live and laugh at it all.

Words and Music by Lew Brown and Ray Henderson
Copyright © 1931 by DeSylva, Brown & Henderson, Inc.
Copyright renewed, assigned to Chappell & Co., Inc.

THE SOUND OF MUSIC

Verse
My day in the hills has come to an end, I know.
A star has come out to tell me it's time to go.
But deep in the dark green shadows are voices that urge me to stay.
So I pause and I wait and I listen for one more sound,
For one more lovely thing the hills might say.

Chorus
The hills are alive with The Sound Of Music,
With songs they have sung for a thousand years.
The hills fill my heart with The Sound Of Music,
My heart wants to sing ev'ry song it hears.
My heart wants to beat
Like the wings of the birds that rise from the lake to the trees,
My heart wants to sigh
Like a chime that flies from a church on a breeze,
To laugh like a brook when it trips and falls over stones on its way,
To sing through the night like a lark who is learning to pray.
I go to the hills when my heart is lonely,
I know I will hear what I've heard before.
My heart will be blessed with The Sound Of Music
And I'll sing once more.

Words by Oscar Hammerstein II   Music By Richard Rodgers
Copyright © 1959 by Richard Rodgers and Oscar Hammerstein II

Williamson Music, Inc., owner of publication and allied rights
for the Western Hemisphere & Japan.

SOMETIMES I'M HAPPY

Verse 1
He: Ev'ry day seems like a year,
      Sweetheart, when you are not near.
She: All that you claim must be true,
      For I'm just the same as you:

Chorus
      Sometimes I'm Happy, sometimes I'm blue,
      My disposition depends on you,
      I never mind the rain from the skies,
      If I can find the sun in your eyes.
      Sometimes I love you, sometimes I hate you,
      But when I hate you, it's 'cause I love you,
      That's how I am, so what can I do?
      I'm happy when I'm with you.

Verse 2
He: Stars are smiling at me from your eyes.
She: Sunbeams now there will be in the skies.
He: Tell me that you will be true!
She: That will all depend on you, dear!

Words by Irving Caesar   Music by Vincent Youmans
© Copyright 1927 by Harms, Inc. Copyright renewed.

LET'S DO IT

Chorus 1
Birds do it, bees do it,
Even educated fleas do it,
Let's Do It, Let's fall in love.
In Spain, the best upper sets do it,
Lithuanians and Letts do it,
Let's Do It, Let's fall in love.
The Dutch in old Amsterdam do it,
Not to mention the Finns,
Folks in Siam do it,
Think of Siamese twins.
Some Argentines without means do it,
People say, in Boston even beans do it,
Let's Do It, let's fall in love.

Chorus 2
Sponges, they say, do it,
Oysters down in Oyster Bay do it,
Let's Do It, let's fall in love.
Cold Cape Cod clams 'gainst their wish do it,
Even lazy jelly fish do it,
Let's Do It, let's fall in love.
Electric eels, I might add, do it,
Though it shocks 'em, I know.
Why ask if shad do it,
Waiter, bring me shad roe.
In shallow shoals, English soles do it,
Goldfish in the privacy of bowls do it,
Let's Do It, let's fall in love.

Words and Music by Cole Porter
© Copyright 1928 by Harms, Inc. Copyright renewed 1954.

Songs of Religion and Christmas

A nation's religious beliefs are reflected in its music. And a country whose coins are imprinted with the premise "In God We Trust" would naturally be a country that would provide the world with some of its greatest religious songs.

"Rock Of Ages," one early example of America's rich heritage, was composed by two Americans in 1832, and the famous "Nearer, My God, To Thee" followed only a short time later. Both of these are standard musical offerings in churches throughout the United States—and probably always will be.

Early Negro spirituals have contributed their legacy to America's religious music, too. Today's popular gospel music, for example, had its beginning on the plantations of the South in the 1830s, and some of the songs that were sung on these plantations are still being sung today. Although new rhythms give them a contemporary sound and the recording industry gives them a newfound popularity, the music and the message it imparts have remained basically the same as when these songs were written.

American-inspired Christmas music is of more recent vintage—it was not until the Puritan influence receded in the mid-nineteenth century that there was any need for it. Prior to that time, it was widely held that Christmas was a pagan institution. Finally, it was the ministers who started writing songs for their celebrations.

Yet, each Christmas season, when congregations gather in churches and families gather for reunions, most of the songs that are sung have been created by American songwriters. Whether a robed and surpliced choir is singing "We Three Kings Of Orient Are" or all the grandkids are gathered around the tree to sing "All I Want For Christmas," it's American music that's being sung.

All too often, the enormous popularity and long-lasting fame of a religious song completely overshadow its composer. These are not the name-in-lights writers of the Broadway stage or the screen-credited composers of Hollywood. These are America's great composers who just happen to be less well known than their music. Nonetheless, their work will go on and on—as long as there are churches and as long as there is Christmas.

208

There was a time when to enjoy gospel music you had to take in a prayer
meeting at the nearest fundamentalist church or walk slowly by a tent meeting on
a summer night. Now, praise the Lord, you may hear a gospel song such as
"He's Got The Whole World In His Hands" when you turn on the radio or walk into
a record shop. Gospel music has transcended the purely religious environment
and has developed into a music form to be heard and enjoyed by anyone of any faith.

Old-fashioned gospel music is a blend of the Negro spiritual and the Anglo
hymn, which is indigenous to the United States. In everyday language, it is strictly
American and it's happy music in praise of God.

Whether "He's Got The Whole World In His Hands" is performed by Laurie
London, Marian Anderson, Mahalia Jackson, Roberta Flack, or your own family group,
here's a song that expresses man's belief in a Supreme Being—not in any partisan,
sectarian way, but in an openhearted statement of love.

In many ways, gospel music is American music at its finest—taking something
that had previously been done by rote and expressing it from the heart.

HE'S GOT THE WHOLE WORLD IN HIS HANDS

Adapted by
GEOFF LOVE

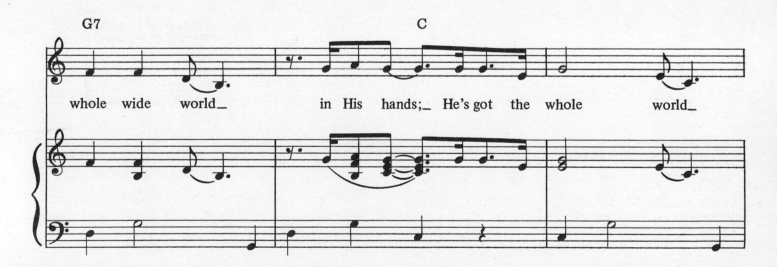

in His hands;___ He's got the whole world in His

hands.

He's got the lil - l ti - ny ba-by in His hands;___ He's got the
He's got___ you and me, broth-er, in His hands;_ He's got___
He's got___ ev - 'ry-bod - y here___ in His hands;_ He's got___

lil - l ti - ny ba - by in His hands,___ He's got the
you and me, sis - ter, in His hands,___ He's got_____
ev - 'ry-bod - y here___ in His hands,___ He's got_____

lit - tle ti - ny ba - by in His hands,___ He's got the
you and me, broth - er, in His hands,___ He's got the
ev - 'ry-bod - y here___ in His hands,___ He's got the

O Little Town of Bethlehem

When you've sung a Christmas carol since your childhood, it's easy to imagine that the hymn must date back to antiquity or to the time of the early Christian church. But that isn't always the case. One of our most loved Christmas hymns, "O Little Town Of Bethlehem," was written in 1868.

The 1860s were turbulent times at best. The Civil War had virtually sapped the strength from the nation and threatened its very existence. Yet, during this stormy period of our nation's history, a surprising amount of church music was created. And even though the stage presentations of the time were the breeding grounds for most of the popular music, religious songs were gaining prominence, too.

Music that reflected the religious views of the times was being spotlighted by such songs as "Lead Kindly Light" and "Sweet By And By," both written in the same year that a Philadelphia minister and his church organist wrote "O Little Town of Bethlehem" for the children's Christmas celebration at Holy Trinity Episcopal Church.

The song was quickly published in a hymnal for church and Sunday schools and was distributed nationally. Since then, it has become a traditional part of the Christmas celebration, not only in the United States but around the world.

When "O Little Town Of Bethlehem" was sung for the first time on Christmas Day, 1868, it seemed to be a harbinger of hope for a war-torn nation. That same day, President Andrew Johnson declared amnesty to all Civil War participants.

"O Little Town Of Bethlehem" was inspired by hope given the world nearly two thousand years before, but its message was equally appropriate for war-ravaged cities of our country, hoping to live again in peace and harmony.

O LITTLE TOWN OF BETHLEHEM

Arranged by Frank Metis

Words and Music by
PHILLIPS BROOKS
LEWIS H. REDNER

Slowly

1. O Lit - tle Town Of Beth - le - hem, How still we_ see thee

lie; A - bove thy deep and dream - less sleep The si - lent_ stars go

by. Yet in thy dark streets shin - eth The ev - er - last - ing

Light; The hopes and fears of all the years Are

met in thee to - night. O night.

2. For Christ is born of Mary,
   And gathered all above,
   While mortals sleep, the angels keep
   Their watch of wondering love.
   O morning stars, together
   Proclaim the holy birth,
   And praises sing to God the King,
   And peace to men on earth.

3. How silently, how silently,
   The wondrous gift is giv'n!
   So God imparts to human hearts
   The blessings of His heav'n.
   No ear may hear His coming,
   But in this world of sin,
   Where meek souls will receive Him still,
   The dear Christ enters in.

When you hear the music, you may well think that "We Three Kings Of Orient Are"
is a Christmas carol that originated during medieval times. Actually,
it isn't a Christmas carol at all, but a hymn for Epiphany, the festival that celebrates
the presentation of Christ to the gentiles in the persons of the Magi—
Kaspar, Melchior, and Balthazar, the three kings who brought gifts to the baby Jesus.
And the song wasn't written in the middle ages, but in 1857.

Both the words and music were the creation of John Henry Hopkins, the son of the
second Bishop of Vermont and rector of Christ Church in Williamsport,
Pennsylvania. As a serious student of music, Hopkins knew that blending the major and
minor modes in his melody would give the hymn an exotic sound.
He did his work so well that for years American critics could not believe that Hopkins
had done anything but arrange a song written in the Middle Ages.

There is only one reminder in this peaceful hymn of the strife wracking 1857 America.
Ever so subtly by the choice of subject, Hopkins reminds carolers that
Christianity never favored racial discrimination—of the three Magi, one was a Negro.

WE THREE KINGS OF ORIENT ARE

Words and Music by
JOHN F. HOPKINS

Arranged by Frank Metis

Moderately slow

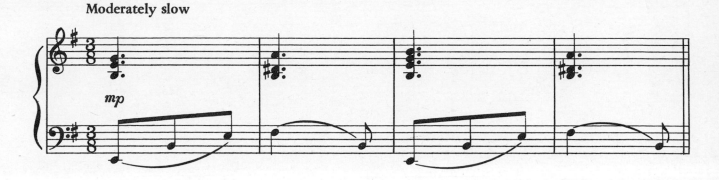

Verse:

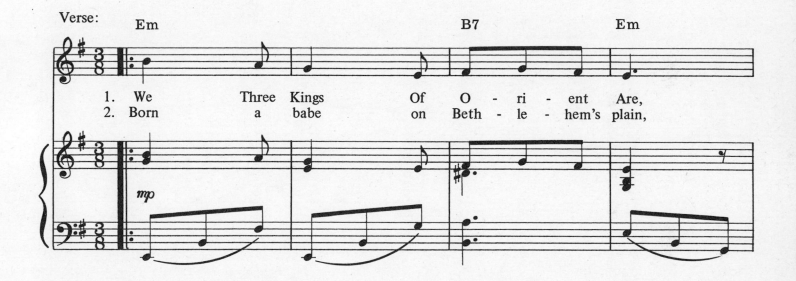

1. We   Three Kings   Of O - ri - ent Are,
2. Born   a babe   on Beth - le - hem's plain,

Bear - ing gifts   we trav - erse far
Gold   we bring   to crown Him a - gain;

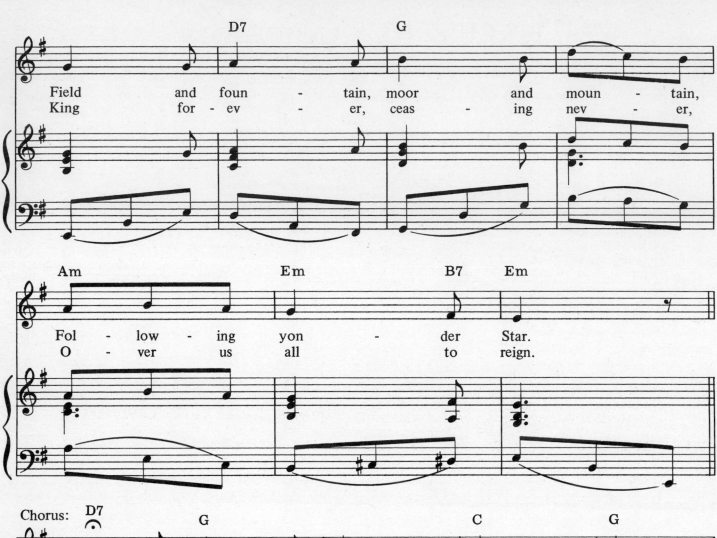

Field   and foun - tain, moor   and moun - tain,
King   for - ev   - er, ceas   - ing nev - er,

Fol - low - ing yon - der Star.
O   - ver   us   all   to reign.

Chorus:

Oh,_____ star   of won - der, star   of might,

Star   with roy - al beau - ty bright,   West - ward

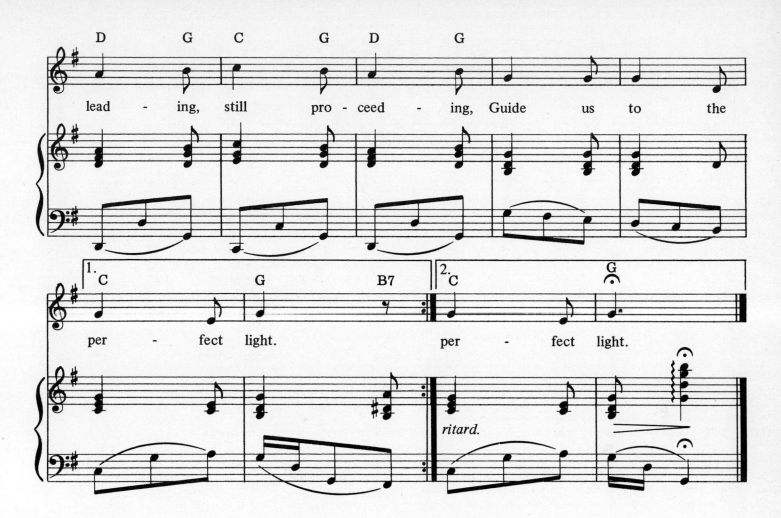

lead - ing, still pro - ceed - ing, Guide us to the

per - fect light. per - fect light.

3. Frankincense to offer have I;
   Incense owns a Deity nigh,
   Pray'r and praising all men raising,
   Worship God on high. (Chorus)

4. Myrrh is mine; its bitter perfume
   Breathes a life of gath'ring gloom;
   Sorrowing, sighing, bleeding, dying,
   Sealed in the stone cold tomb. (Chorus)

5. Glorious now behold Him rise,
   King and God and Sacrifice;
   Heav'n sing "Hallelujah!"
   "Hallelujah!" earth replies. (Chorus)

Other Songs of Religion and Christmas

THE OLD RUGGED CROSS

Verse 1
On a hill far away stood an old rugged cross,
The emblem of suff'ring and shame,
And I love that old cross where the dearest and best
For a world of lost sinners was slain.

Chorus
So I'll cherish The Old Rugged Cross,
Till my trophies at last I lay down;
I will cling to The Old Rugged Cross,
And exchange it some day for a crown.

Verse 2
Oh, that old rugged cross, so despised by the world,
Has a wondrous attraction for me,
For the dear Lamb of God left His glory above,
To bear it to dark Calvary.

Verse 3
In The Old Rugged Cross, stained with blood so divine,
A wondrous beauty I see;
For 'twas on that old cross Jesus suffered and died,
To pardon and sanctify me.

Verse 4
To The Old Rugged Cross I will ever be true,
Its shame and reproach gladly bear;
Then He'll call me some day to my home far away,
Where His glory forever I'll share.

Words and Music by George Bennard

GOD BLESS THE CHILD

Them that's got shall get, them that's not shall lose,
So the Bible said, and it still is news;
Mama may have, Papa may have,
But God Bless The Child that's got his own! That's got his own.
Yes, the strong gets more, while the weak ones fade,
Empty pockets don't ever make the grade,
Mama may have, Papa may have,
But God Bless The Child that's got his own! That's got his own.
Money, you got lots o' friends, crowdin' 'round the door,
When you're gone and spendin' ends, they don't come no more.
Rich relations give, crust of bread, and such,
You can help yourself, but don't take too much!
Mama may have, Papa may have,
But God Bless The Child that's got his own! That's got his own.

Words and Music by Arthur Herzog, Jr. and Billie Holiday

© Copyright 1941 Edward B. Marks Music Corp. Copyright renewed.

ROCK OF AGES

Rock Of Ages, cleft for me,
Let me hide myself in Thee;
Let the water and the blood
From Thy wounded side which flow'd,
Be of sin the double cure,
Save from wrath and make me pure.

Could my tears forever flow,
Could my zeal no languor know,
These for sin could not atone;
Thou must save, and Thou alone:
In my hand no price I bring,
Simply to Thy cross I cling.

While I draw this fleeting breath,
When my eyes shall close in death,
When I rise to worlds unknown,
And behold Thee on Thy Throne,
Rock Of Ages, cleft for me,
Let me hide myself in Thee.

Words by Augustus M. Toplady   Music by Thomas Hastings

NEARER, MY GOD, TO THEE

Nearer, my God, to Thee, Nearer to Thee!
E'en tho' it be a cross that raiseth me;
Still all my song shall be, Nearer, my God, to Thee,
Nearer, my God, to Thee, Nearer to Thee.

Tho' like the wanderer, the sun gone down,
Darkness be over me, my rest a stone,
Yet in my dreams I'd be, Nearer, my God, to Thee
Nearer, my God, to Thee, Nearer to Thee.

There let the way appear, steps unto heav'n;
All that Thou sendest me, in mercy giv'n;
Angels to beckon me Nearer, my God, to Thee,
Nearer, my God, to Thee, Nearer to Thee.

Then, when my waking tho'ts bright with Thy praise,
Out of my stony griefs Bethel I'll raise;
So by my woes to be Nearer, my God, to Thee,
Nearer, my God, to Thee, Nearer to Thee.

Words by Sarah F. Adams   Music by Lowell Mason

CATHEDRAL IN THE PINES

Daddy wore a happy smile,
When his bride came down the aisle,
In that little old Cathedral In The Pines.
When a baby filled their nest,
He was taken to be blessed
In that little old Cathedral In The Pines.
He grew up and joined the choir,
Where the organ played each day.
And he found his heart's desire,
In a girl who came to pray.
Once again the wedding bells will softly peal,
And while you and I before the altar kneel,
I will hold your hand in mine,
As they did in Auld Lang Syne,
In that little old Cathedral In The Pines.

Words and Music by Charles and Nick Kenny
© Copyright 1938 by Bourne Co.
New York, N.Y. Copyright renewed.

ALL I WANT FOR CHRISTMAS IS MY TWO FRONT TEETH

Verse
Ev'rybody stops and stares at me,
These two teeth are gone as you can see.
I don't know just who to blame for this catastrophe!
But my one wish on Christmas Eve is as plain as it can be!

Chorus
All I Want For Christmas Is My Two Front Teeth,
My two front teeth, see my two front teeth!
Gee, if I could only have my two front teeth,
Then I could wish you, "Merry Christmas."
It seems so long since I could say,
"Sister Susie sitting on a thistle!"
Gosh oh gee, how happy I'd be,
If I could only whistle (thhh.)
All I Want For Christmas Is My Two Front Teeth,
My two front teeth, see my two front teeth.
Gee, if I could only have my two front teeth,
Then I could wish you "Merry Christmas!"

Words and Music by Don Gardner
© Copyright 1946 & 1948 by M. Witmark & Sons

SIMPLE SONG OF LOVE

Jesus called the twelve who'd been with him,
Half hoping they would help Him to forget His fears,
Missing them now it was near the end
Of all the things they shared together through the years.

Standing with a sadness in His heart
He took His leave of all the friends He'd come to know.
Leaving them a sign in bread and wine,
He spoke and told them all the things they had to know.

Won't you sing a Simple Song Of Love
And let the spirit lead where it may take you to.
Talk with all the people ev'rywhere
And let them see there's love in ev'rything you do.

Remember Me always for today
Though I must leave and go away from you.
He said He'd send another before long
And they must believe although they would not see.
Although though He'd be gone, they're not alone,
Believe in this if you believe in Me.

Then He said there's something I can see
That one of you, My friends, today will Me betray.
But they exclaimed, and said, Lord, it's not me,
You know that we will stand beside you come what may.

Won't you sing a Simple Song Of Love
And let the spirit lead where it may take you to.
Talk with all the people ev'rywhere,
And let them see there's love in ev'rything you do.

Remember Me always for today,
Though I must leave, yet I will stay always,
Won't you sing a Simple Song Of Love,
And let the spirit lead where it may take you to.
Talk with all the people ev'rywhere,
And let them see there's love in ev'rything you do.

Words and Music by Larry Hogan
© Copyright 1972 by Larry Hogan. Copyright assigned to ARAT Music, 1974.

JOY TO THE WORLD

Joy To The World! The Lord is come; Let earth receive her King;
Let ev'ry heart prepare Him room, and heav'n and nature sing,
And heav'n and nature sing, And heav'n, and heav'n and nature sing.

Joy To The World! The Savior reigns; Let men their songs employ;
While fields and floods, rock, hills and plains, repeat the sounding joy,
Repeat the sounding joy, Repeat, repeat the sounding joy.

No more let sin and sorrow grow, Nor thorns infest the ground;
He comes to make His blessings flow, Far as the curse is found,
Far as the curse is found, Far as, far as the curse is found.

He rules the world with truth and grace, And makes the nations prove
The glories of His righteousness, And wonders of His love,
And wonders of His love, And wonders, and wonders of His love.

Words by Isaac Watts   Music by George F. Handel

Songs of Humor

America has been laughing at herself in song ever since the early
1800s, a heyday for parodies of English songs such as "The
Cork Leg," which concerned a Dutch merchant whose artificial leg ran
away with him. After that, the minstrel shows and the
vaudeville stage made novelty songs flourish. Composers would write
songs about almost anything—the war of the sexes,
immigrants, Negroes, and history. And sometimes, they'd just
put gibberish to music.

Every era had its favorite object of fun. Starting in the 1840s with
the rise in popularity of the blackface minstrel show, there
were songs such as "Zip Coon," who was to succeed Andrew Jackson
as President. Audiences roared—and made up parodies such
as "Turkey In The Straw." "Polly Wolly Doodle" was another silly tune
that delighted audiences of the day.

People kept on laughing as the minstrel show gave way to
vaudeville. Nonsense songs got laughs as never before
in the nineties: witness "Zizzy, Ze Zum, Zum" of 1898. "Ta-ra-ra-bom-
de-ray" was first sung in 1891 in St. Louis by Mama Lou,
who presided over Babe Connor's chandeliered restaurant in the
costume later made famous by Aunt Jemima. In burlesque,
vaudeville's female-studded cousin, second- and third-generation
Dutchmen, Irishmen, Italians, Chinese, and Greeks would
roar at the escapades of more recent immigrants.

The twenties, more earnest about having a good time than any
other era up to then, was another big decade for nonsense
songs. In fact, it went nonsense-happy just as it had gone dance-crazy.
"Yes! We Have No Bananas," a tune introduced by its
originators Frank Silver and Irving Cohn in 1923, is acknowledged as
the most successful nonsense song of all time. It had
competitors—"Diga, Diga, Doo," "I'm Wild About Horns On
Automobiles That Go Ta-ta-ta-ta," and "I Love To
Dunk A Hunk Of Sponge Cake," along with lighthearted pieces such
as "Baby Face" and "I'm Looking Over A Four Leaf Clover."

During the Depression, soup lines, closed banks, and labor-
management disputes made the outlook for the future black
indeed, but those were the very same years that audiences chuckled
through "Who's Afraid Of The Big Bad Wolf?" and
"Jeepers Creepers." Plainly, America's funnybone is durable indeed.

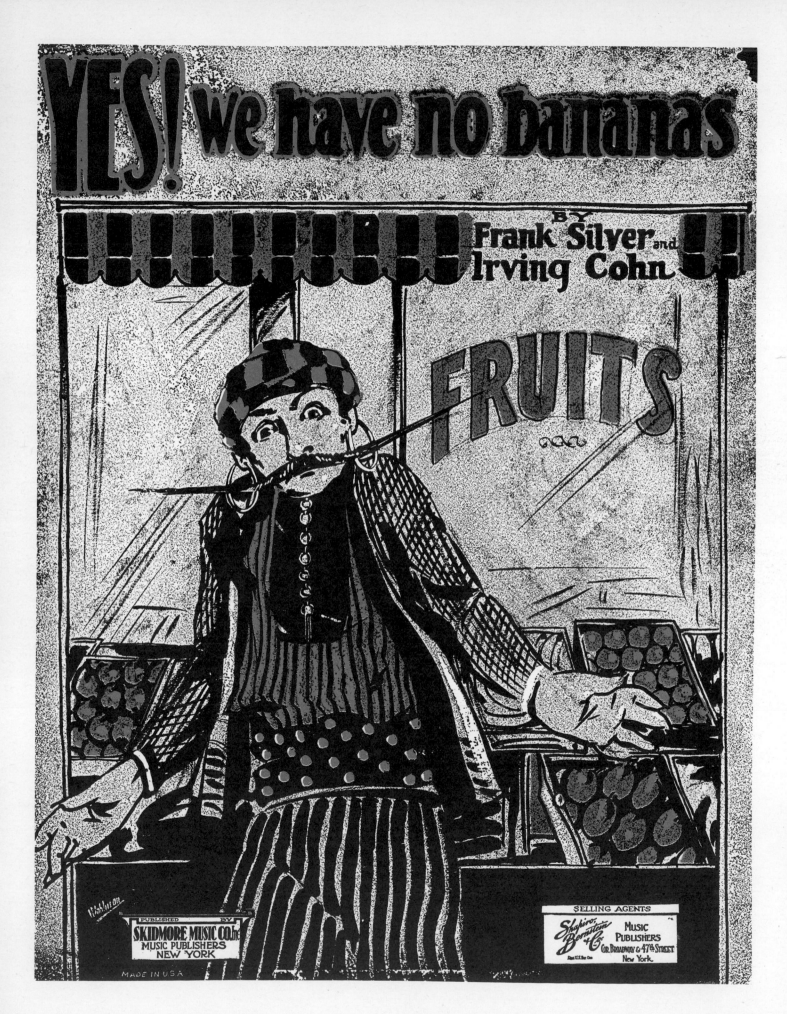

Yes! We Have No Bananas

Songwriters Frank Silver and Irving Cohn actually heard a Greek fruit dealer say this to a customer one day in 1923, and they later turned the remark into one of the most successful nonsense songs ever published. The melody is a rare concoction of Handel's "Hallelujah Chorus," Balfe's "I Dreamt That I Dwelt In Marble Halls," "An Old-Fashioned Garden," and "My Bonnie"—a hodgepodge just like the grammar. Humorists have pointed out that if you were to sing the original words to the succession of songs whose tunes are incorporated, you'd be singing this: "Hallelujah, Bananas! Oh bring back my Bonnie to me. I dreamt that I dwelt in marble halls—the kind you seldom see. I was seeing Nellie home, to an old fashioned garden; but Hallelujah, Bananas! Oh bring back my Bonnie to me!"

Even in the Cohn-Silver version, "Bananas" is so plainly crazy that when the songwriters introduced the new piece, first at a Long Island roadhouse and later at Murray's Restaurant in New York City, audiences were stunned by the musical freak. And, the general public was anything but anxious to accept it as a popular song.

At about the same time, Eddie Cantor was in Philadelphia for out-of-town tryouts with his musical *Make It Snappy*. He was looking for something to jazz up the show, and when he added "Yes! We Have No Bananas" at the Wednesday matinee, the audiences went into hysterics. They made him repeat the chorus for more than 15 minutes.

From then on, Cantor made "Bananas" a permanent part of his act, recorded it for Victor, and put it on the sound track of the 1954 *Eddie Cantor Story*—and it has been getting chuckles from everyone who hears it ever since.

YES! WE HAVE NO BANANAS

By FRANK SILVER
and IRVING COHN

Moderately

Verse:

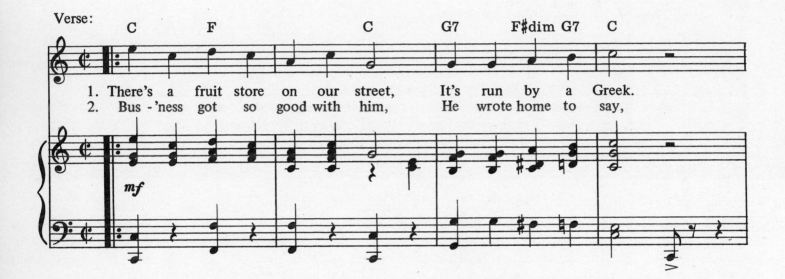

1. There's a fruit store on our street, It's run by a Greek.
2. Bus-'ness got so good with him, He wrote home to say,

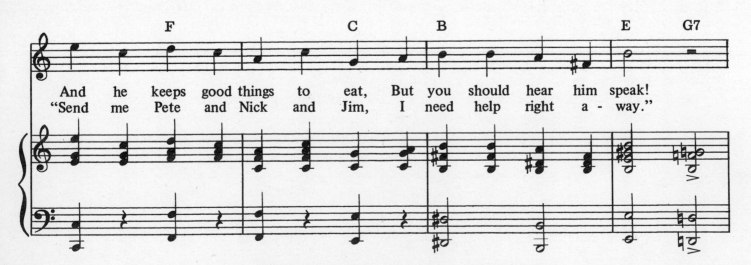

And he keeps good things to eat, But you should hear him speak!
"Send me Pete and Nick and Jim, I need help right a-way."

Is - land po - TAH - to, _____ But

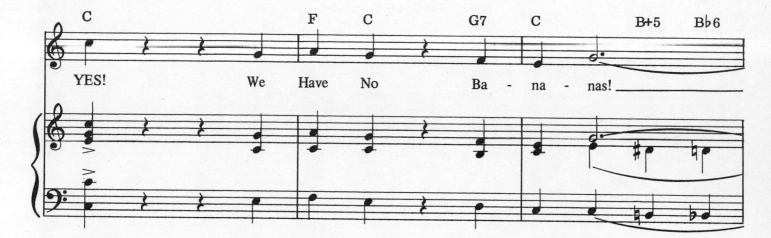

YES! We Have No Ba - na - nas! _____

We have no ba - na - nas to -

day.

day. _____

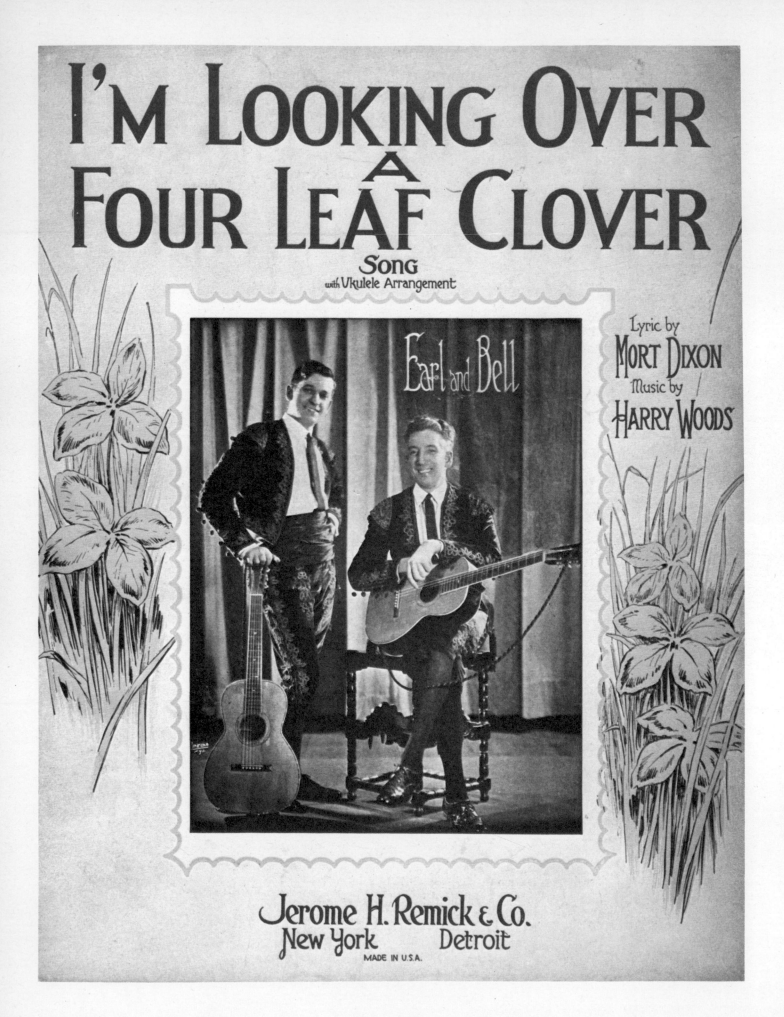

Al "Jazzbeaux" Collins

I'm Looking Over a Four Leaf Clover

Some songs can barely be heard over the gales of laughter they generate; others are just plain happy songs that make audiences want to kick up their heels and forget their troubles, if only for a little while. But both are part of the lighter side of American music.

One of the happiest songs ever written is "I'm Looking Over A Four Leaf Clover," introduced in 1927 by songwriters Mort Dixon and Harry Woods. Part of the reason this song is a standard today is because it was involved in one of the most bizarre bits of radio promotion ever experienced by the American listening public.

Twenty-one years after the song was originally published, a new recording by Art Mooney was released. A disc jockey in Salt Lake City by the name of Al "Jazzbeaux" Collins played it on the air and then started to get calls from listeners requesting another airing of the toe-tapping tune. Collins responded by playing the song over and over again—for nearly 24 hours nonstop.

Both protest and praise came from listeners, but the crazy stunt got national news coverage, and "I'm Looking Over A Four Leaf Clover" was an overnight best seller.

Several generations of Americans have been entertained by the bouncy melody and heart-lifting lyrics of this song, which expresses so successfully what the French call *joie de vivre*—the joy of living.

Songs that invite audiences to let their hair down and enjoy themselves can go a long way toward countering the "blues." These songs, like escapist movies, give people a few minutes respite from their problems. And there's definitely nothing wrong with doing that.

I'M LOOKING OVER A FOUR LEAF CLOVER

Lyric by
MORT DIXON

Music by
HARRY WOODS

On - ly wait till I com -mu - ni - cate,

Here's just what I'll say: _____

Chorus:

I'm Look - ing O - ver A Four Leaf Clo -

- ver that I o - ver - looked be - fore; _____

One leaf is sun - shine, the sec - ond is rain,___

Third is the ros - es that grow in the lane,___

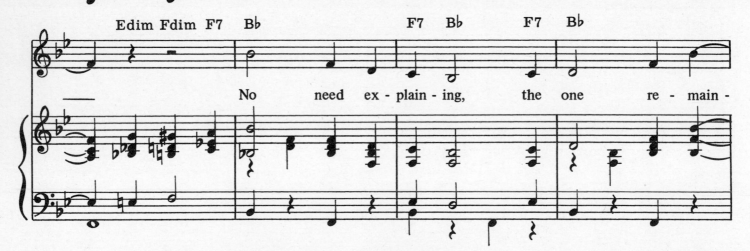

No need ex - plain - ing, the one re - main -

- ing is some - bod - y I a - dore.___

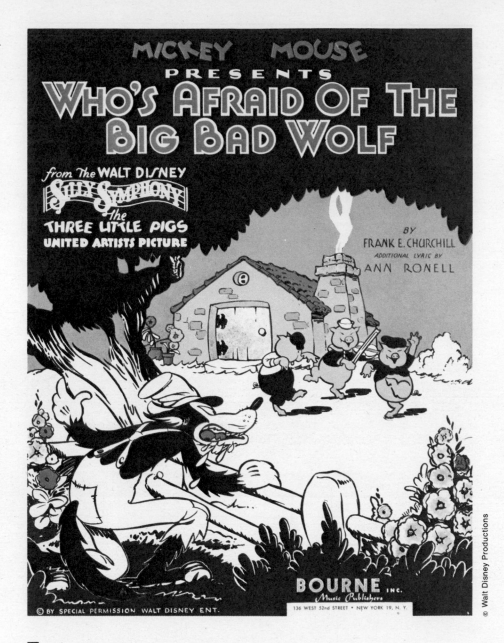

Even during the Depression, there was a place for fun songs. In 1933, our nation was singing, humming, and whistling a silly song from the animation of a children's story. "Who's Afraid Of The Big Bad Wolf?" was getting just as much attention as the Jeanette MacDonald-Nelson Eddy songs of the day.

The song was written by Frank Churchill and Ann Ronell as the key theme for Walt Disney's animated cartoon, *The Three Little Pigs.* Disney was a master of integrating music with his animations to create an overall effect—a combination that has thrilled audiences all over the world.

"Who's Afraid Of The Big Bad Wolf?" was granted its passport early in the game and was translated into many languages as the cartoon traveled to movie screens in other countries. The song and the movie were great ambassadors of America and were well received everywhere. Russia, in fact, claimed to have identified "Who's Afraid Of The Big Bad Wolf?" as a Soviet folk song.

In 1961, the talented Barbra Streisand used this same song to introduce her professional debut in a Greenwich Village nightclub. This proves, in context or out, sung for small fry or adults, in America or the far reaches of the globe, "Who's Afraid Of The Big Bad Wolf?" is one of the all-time great hits when what's called for is music—just for the fun of it.

WHO'S AFRAID OF THE BIG BAD WOLF?

Additional Lyric by
ANN RONELL

Words and Music by
FRANK E. CHURCHILL

Slowly

Chorus:

Who's A-fraid Of The Big Bad Wolf,   big bad wolf,   big bad wolf?

Who's A-fraid Of The Big Bad Wolf? Tra la la la la.   la. 1. Long a-
                                                           (Came the)

Verse:

go, there were three pigs, Lit-tle hand-some pig-gy-wigs, For the big bad, very big,
2. day when fate did frown, And the wolf blew in-to town, With a gruff "puff,puff," he

very bad— wolf, They— did-n't give three figs. Num-ber One was ver-y
puffed just e-nough, And the hay house fell right down. One and Two were scared to

gay, And he built his house with hay; With a hey-hey toot, he
death, Of the big bad wolf-ie's breath; "By the hair of your chin-ny-chin,

Chorus:

Who's A - fraid Of The Big Bad Wolf, big bad wolf, big bad wolf?

Who's A - fraid Of The Big Bad Wolf, Tra la la la la.

Who's A - fraid Of The Big Bad Wolf, big bad wolf, big bad wolf?

Who's A - fraid Of The Big Bad Wolf? Tra la la la la. 2. Came the la.

BABY FACE

Words and Music by
BENNY DAVIS
and
HARRY AKST

WHEN PERFORMING THIS COMPOSITION KINDLY GIVE ALL
PROGRAM CREDITS TO

Remick
MUSIC CORPORATION
NEW YORK, N.Y.

Price 50¢
in U.S.A.

Baby Face

Sometimes, the thing that makes a song humorous, or happy,
or lighthearted is its ability to say almost nothing,
yet, at the same time, sound profound. "Baby Face" is that kind
of song. No music is happier, no music makes you
feel better. But, on studying the lyrics, you'll find it's just
a nonsensical song about someone called "Baby Face."

The Benny Davis and Harry Akst song was written in 1926
when the most enviable "baby face" around was that
of actress Clara Bow—the "It" girl. Faces of the twenties spotlighted
cupid bow lips, heavily shadowed eyes framed by
thin-lined penciled brows, and the inevitable beauty spot,
either pasted on or painted on in some glamourously
conspicuous spot. Girls who might have inspired a song such
as "Baby Face" probably spent their time doing crossword
puzzles or playing Mah-Jongg, the two popular pastimes of the
twenties. Or they may have cheered on participants
in marathon races, flagpole sitting, or goldfish-eating contests.
And after dark, they would have headed for a ballroom
to do the Charleston, which had been the latest thing since 1923.

But the song was popular a second time with its revival
in 1947—and 1947 wasn't the same sort of easygoing
period. Or was it? Nonsense obviously had its place in the 40s,
too. These were the days of wrestling matches and roller
derbies, pyramid clubs and chain letters, and postwar girlie
promotional stunts. Maybe "Baby Face" is a song that
could have been written anytime.

The female faces that might have inspired this tune have
changed over the years, but the lilting happiness of
"Baby Face" is definitely more lasting than the passing fads
in fashions, cosmetics, or hairstyles.

BABY FACE

Words and Music by
BENNY DAVIS and
HARRY AKST

Moderately

Verse:

Ros - y cheeks and turn'd up nose and curl - y hair, _____
When you were a ba - by not so long a - go, _____

I'm rav - ing 'bout my ba - by now. _____
You must have been the cut - est thing. _____

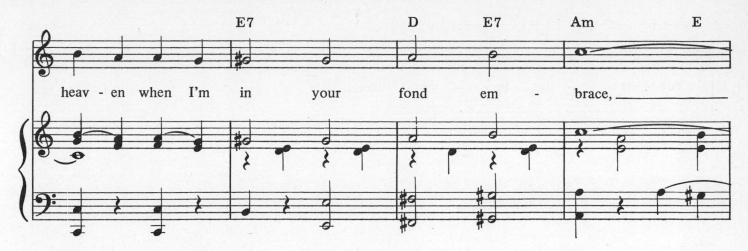

heav - en when I'm in your fond em - brace, ____

____ I did -n't need a shove ___ 'Cause I just fell in love ___

____ With your pret - ty Ba - by

Face. ____

Face. ____

More Happy Tunes

DON'T BRING LULU

Verse
"Your presence is requested," wrote little Johnny Whit,
But with this invitation, There is a stipulation:
When you attend this party,
You'll all be treated right.
But there's a wild and woolly woman
You boys can't invite. Now...

Chorus
You can bring Pearl, she's a darn nice girl,
But Don't Bring Lulu!
You can bring Rose with the turned up nose,
But Don't Bring Lulu!
Lulu always wants to do
What we boys don't want her to.
When she struts her stuff around,
London Bridge is falling down.
You can bring cake or porterhouse steak,
But Don't Bring Lulu!
Lulu gets blue and she goes "coo-koo"
Like the clock upon the shelf.
She's the kind of smarty
Who breaks up every party.
Hullabalooloo.
Don't bring Lulu. I'll bring her myself!

Words by Billy Rose and Lew Brown   Music by Ray Henderson
© Copyright 1925 by Jerome H. Remick & Co. Copyright renewed.

DANCE WITH A DOLLY

Verse
As I was walkin' down the street,
Down the street, down the street,
I met somebody who was mighty sweet,
Mighty fair to see.
I asked her would she like to have a talk,
Have a talk, make some talk,
All the fellows standin' on the walk,
Wishin' they were me:

Chorus
Mamma, Mamma, let me dress up tonight,
Dress up tonight, dress up tonight,
I've got a secret, gonna 'fess up tonight,
Gonna dance by the light of the moon.
Gonna Dance With A Dolly with a hole in her stockin'
While our knees keep a knockin'
And our toes keep a rockin'.
Dance With A Dolly with a hole in her stockin',
Dance by the light of the moon.

Words and Music by Terry Shand, Jimmy Eaton, and Mickey Leader
Copyright © 1940 and 1944 by
Shapiro, Bernstein & Co., Inc. Copyrights renewed.

HOW YA' GONNA KEEP 'EM DOWN ON THE FARM?

Verse
"Reuben, Reuben, I've been thinking," said his wifey dear
"Now that all is peaceful and calm,
The boys will soon be back on the farm."
Mister Reuben started winking, and slowly rubbed his chin;
He pulled his chair up close to mother,
And he asked her with a grin:

Chorus
How 'Ya Gonna Keep 'Em Down On The Farm,
After they've seen Paree?
How 'ya gonna keep 'em away from Broadway,
Jazzin' a-roun' and paintin' the town?
How 'ya gonna keep 'em away from harm?
That's a mystery;
They'll never want to see a rake or plow,
And who the deuce can parley vous a cow?
How 'Ya Gonna Keep 'Em Down On The Farm,
After they've seen Paree?

Words by Sam M. Lewis and Joe Young   Music by Walter Donaldson
© Copyright 1919 by Mills Music, Inc.
Copyright Renewed 1947 by Mills Music, Inc. and Warock Music, Inc.

BALLIN' THE JACK

Verse
Folks in Georgia's 'bout to go insane,
Since that new dance down in Georgia came;
I'm the only person who's to blame,
I'm the party introduced it there, So!
Give me credit to know a thing or two,
Give me credit for springing something new;
I will show this little dance to you,
When I do you'll say that it's a bear.

Chorus
First you put your two knees close up tight,
Then you sway 'em to the left, then you sway 'em to the right,
Step around the floor kind of nice and light,
Then you twis' around and twis' around with all your might,
Stretch your lovin' arms straight out in space,
Then you do the Eagle Rock with style and grace,
Swing your foot way 'round then bring it back,
Now that's what I call "Ballin' The Jack."

Words by Jim Burris   Music by Chris Smith
© Copyright 1913 by Edward B. Marks Music Corp. Copyright renewed.

SAM, YOU MADE THE PANTS TOO LONG

Verse
Trousers dragging, slowly dragging thru the street,
Yes! I'm walking, but I'm walking without feet;
I'm not finding fault at all,
You're too big and I'm too small,
But Sam, you promised me both ends would meet,

Chorus
You made the coat and vest fit the best,
You made the lining nice and strong;
But Sam, You Made The Pants Too Long.
You made the peak lapel look so swell,
So who am I to say you're wrong?
But Sam, You Made The Pants Too Long.
They got a belt and they got suspenders,
So what can they lose?
But what good are belts and what good suspenders,
When the pants are hanging over the shoes.
You feel a winter breeze up and down the knees,
The belt is where the tie belongs;
'Cause Sam, Sam, Sam, You Made The Pants Too Long!

Adapted from "Lord, You Made The Night Too Long" by Sam M. Lewis and Victor Young
Words by Fred Whitehouse and Milton Berle

Copyright © 1932 and 1940 by Shapiro, Bernstein & Co. Copyrights renewed.

Copyright 1966 by Shapiro, Bernstein & Co., Inc.

HOLD TIGHT—HOLD TIGHT
(Want Some Sea Food Mama)

Verse
There is a pedlar from Cincinnati
Who comes daily with his fishery.
Fish is what he sells.
Listen to him and hear him yell, "Fish!"

Chorus
Hold Tight, Hold Tight, Hold Tight, Hold Tight.
Foo-ra-de-ack-a-sa-ki, Want Some Sea Food Mama.
Shrimps and rice—they're very nice.
Hold Tight, Hold Tight, Hold Tight, Hold Tight.
Foo-ra-de-ack-a-sa-ki, Want Some Sea Food Mama.
Codfish and sauce, and then of course
I like oysters, lobsters too,
I like kippers, mack'rel too,
And I like my tasty bit of fish.
When I come home from work at night,
I get my favorite dish, Fish!
Hold Tight, Hold Tight, Hold Tight, Hold Tight.
Foo-ra-de-ack-a-sa-ki, Want Some Sea Food Mama.
Shrimps and rice, They're very nice! They're very nice!

Words and Music by Kent Brandow, Joseph Miller, and Robinson Ware Spotswood

© Copyright 1939 by American Academy of Music, Inc. Copyright renewed 1967.

PUT YOUR SHOES ON, LUCY

Put Your Shoes On, Lucy, don't-cha know you're in the city,
Put Your Shoes On, Lucy, it's really such a pity
That Lucy can't go barefoot wherever she goes,
'Cause she loves to feel the wiggle of her toes.
Put Your Shoes On, Lucy, 'cause you're here in ol' New York,
You'll get by all righty if you let 'em hear you talk,
All the city slickers love that Southern drawl,
So give 'em that "Honey chile" an' "Hi' you awl."
Lucy, let the good things happen; Lucy, won't ya stop that gappin',
How you act will be the death of me,
Don't they have skyscrapers down in Tennessee?
Put Your Shoes On, Lucy, even tho' they kind-a pinch,
Stop balkin', ya gotta do some walkin', that's a cinch.
Use your party manners, you'll need them and how,
Put Your Shoes On, Lucy, you're a big girl now.

Words and Music by Hank Fort

© Copyright 1947 by Bourne Co., New York, N.Y. Copyright renewed.

JEEPERS CREEPERS

Verse
I don't care what the weatherman says,
When the weatherman says it's raining,
You'll never hear me complaining,
I'm certain the sun will shine,
I don't care how the weather vane points,
When the weather vane points to gloomy,
It's gotta be sunny to me,
When your eyes look into mine.

Chorus
Jeepers Creepers! Where'd ya get those peepers?
Jeepers Creepers! Where'd ya get those eyes?
Gosh all git up! How'd they get so lit up?
Gosh all git up! How'd they get that size?
Golly gee! When you turn those heaters on,
Woe is me! Got to put my cheaters on.
Jeepers Creepers! Where'd ya get those peepers?
Oh! those weepers! How they hypnotize!
Where'd ya get those eyes?

Words by Johnny Mercer   Music by Harry Warren

© Copyright 1938 by M. Witmark & Sons. Copyright renewed.

Songs of Country

Regional music has always flourished in America. But for a long time, ragtime and spirituals belonged to the black community, and hillbilly music only to the mountain people. Cowboy music was what they sang in the West. But as communications improved, regional music started spreading. In 1811, for example, steamboats started bringing Northerners into touch with spirituals and work songs of the Negro laborers. The northern magazines of the day marveled at the strange and wonderful music and dances, and eventually ragtime made its way north. In 1917, five years before Henry Creamer and Turner Layton wrote "Way Down Yonder In New Orleans," the New Orleans red-light district, where jazz had flourished, was closed down by authorities, and all the great jazz men drifted to Chicago and New York, bringing new rhythms, which soon became an integral part of the popular music of the day.

The hillbilly sound had an easier time getting out of the rural pockets of the South where it had originated. At first, it came up on the coattails of traveling medicine shows, but it had no particular appeal to the music-buying public until the advent of radio. During the 1920s, when southern broadcasting stations featured live country music, the hillbilly sound finally left its birthplace.

Essentially the same thing happened in the 1930s to the West's roundup songs. A young composer named Billy Hill, who had spent a baker's dozen years in Utah and Montana, made a successful career of writing cowboy songs such as "Wagon Wheels." And it was during the thirties' vogue for things western that Franklin Delano Roosevelt revived the 1858 "Yellow Rose Of Texas." During this same period, a movement called western swing came to public attention, towing "San Antonio Rose" and composer Bob Wills to popularity with it.

As the ragtime beat found its way into jazz, the western and hillbilly sounds ended up in country-and-western music, which grew by leaps and bounds as big recording studios moved into Nashville. In the course of things, folk singers such as Bob Dylan recorded their albums there and picked up some of the local twang. At the same time, performers such as Roger Miller built their fame on the new sophistication all the activity has brought to the country-western field.

San Antonio Rose

Songwriter-musician Bob Wills and his famous song, "San Antonio Rose" were both products of a movement in country music called "western swing." Although not nationally popular until the late thirties, western swing had been enjoying a strong following in the rural pockets of the United States. And as early as the 1920s, Bob Wills, a fiddler, and Herman Arnspiger, a guitarist, were displaying their brand of music at house parties around Fort Worth, Texas. Soon, the duo was joined by a vocalist by the name of Milton Brown, and the nucleus of the famous Aladdin's Laddies had been formed.

Over the years, the size of the band and its personnel changed, but Bob Wills' style continued to permeate the music. By the 1940s, the group had been permanently titled Bob Wills and the Texas Playboys—and without knowing it, the group was on the verge of becoming nationally famous.

Fame came as a result of "San Antonio Rose." It was recorded first as a country instrumental in November, 1938, then re-recorded with lyrics in 1940. But the song was still just moderately successful. Then, in 1941, Bing Crosby recorded "San Antonio Rose" and the rest is history. In one month, 84,000 copies of the record had been sold, and Bob Wills' song, as well as his particular style of country music, was in the national spotlight.

"San Antonio Rose" was the beginning of Bob Wills' success story. Now, his name is synonymous with the best of America's western music, and his influence is felt on the whole field of country music. It's safe to say that there's not a country and western musician or singer who does not have Bob Wills' songs in his repertoire.

SAN ANTONIO ROSE

Words and Music by
BOB WILLS

Chorus:

Deep with - in my heart lies a mel - o - dy, A

song of old San An - tone. _____ Where in dreams I

live with a mem - o - ry, Be - neath the stars all a -

lone. _____ It was there I found be -

side the Al - a - mo, En - chant - ment strange as the blue up a -

bove. A moon - lit pass that on - ly she would know, Still

hears my bro-ken song of love._____

Moon in all your splen-dor, know on - ly my heart,

Call back my Rose, Rose of San An - tone.

Lips so sweet and ten-der, like pet-als fall-ing a-part,___

Speak once a - gain of my love, my own. Bro - ken

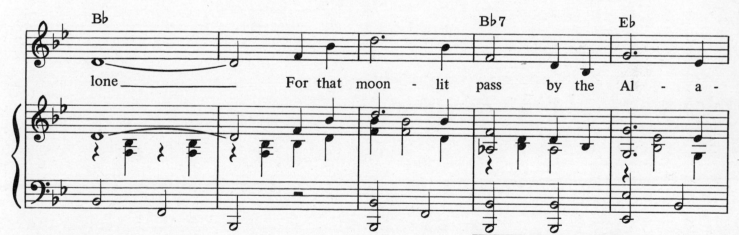

song, emp - ty words I know Still live in my heart all a -

lone _____ For that moon - lit pass by the Al - a -

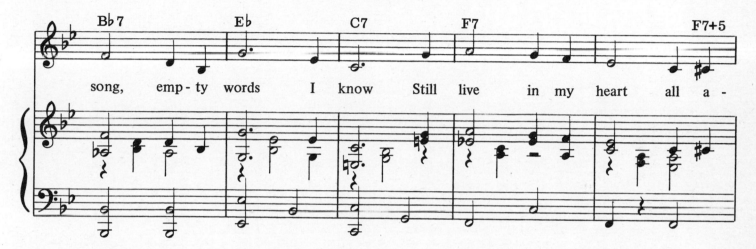

mo, And Rose, my Rose of San An - tone. _____ Deep with - —

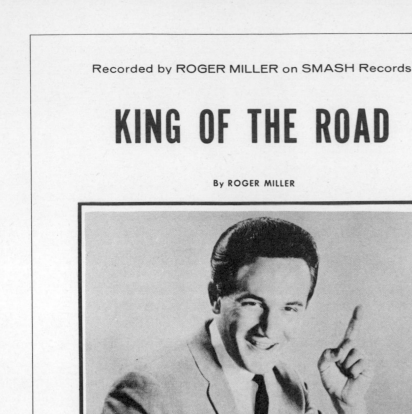

Recorded by ROGER MILLER on SMASH Records

KING OF THE ROAD

By ROGER MILLER

75¢

Tree Publishing Co.,Inc.

04381

An easygoing hobo is hardly who you'd think of as a national hero, yet in 1965, Roger Miller's "King Of The Road" was one of the country's most familiar and best-loved characters. In that year, the song won a total of six "Grammy" awards from the National Academy of Recording Arts and Sciences. The song also won the hearts of every listener it reached.

For years before this success, Roger Miller had been striving for recognition as a performer. He had written material for other stars and had seen it rise on the charts, but he couldn't do the same thing with his own records. Then, with his compositions and recordings of "Dang Me" and "King Of The Road," Roger Miller was established as one of America's best country artists.

Miller's songs are certainly some of the best of today's country music, yet the composer himself evokes an image that's not exactly that of a rough-hewn rural singer. Miller is more the cool hipster, who is as much at home with a network television audience as with the folks at the corner truckstop.

Roger Miller's finely honed sense of rhythm and his catchy lyrics made "King Of The Road" an overwhelming success. And unlike the hobo songs of the twenties, which depicted impoverished, harassed characters, "King Of The Road" glamorizes its hero and makes his strange kind of freedom enviable to anyone who is caught up in the world of the establishment.

KING OF THE ROAD

Words and Music by
ROGER MILLER

1. Trail - er___ for sale or rent;___ Rooms___ to let, ___
2. Third box___ car, mid - night train:___ Des - ti - na - tion
3. Trail - er___ for sale or rent; ___ Rooms___ to let, ___

fif - ty cents;___ No phone,___ no pool, no pets; ___
Ban - gor, Maine.___ Old worn___ out suit and shoes; ___
fif - ty cents; ___ No phone, ___ no pool, no pets;

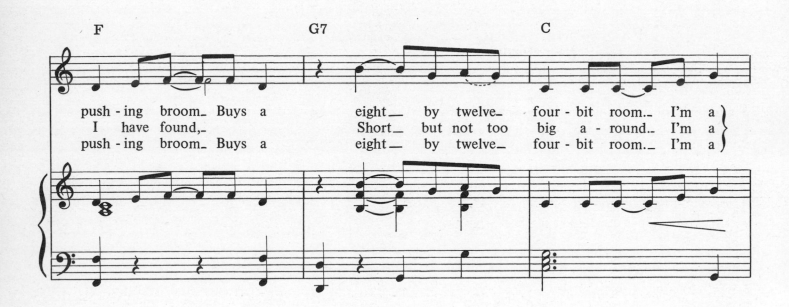

Road.   I know Road.   ev - er - y   en - gi - neer on

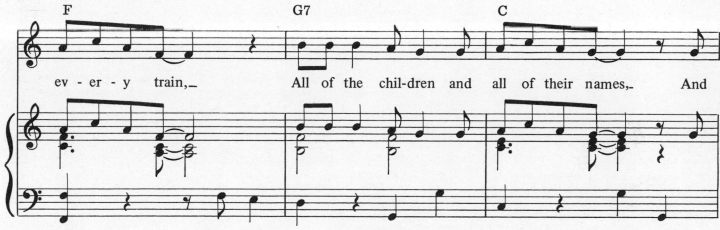

ev - er - y   train,__   All of the chil-dren and   all of their names,__   And

ev - er - y   hand - out   in   ev - er - y   town,__   And

ev - 'ry   lock   that   ain't locked   when   no   one's   a - round.   3. I   sing . . .

When Tin Pan Alley discovered that there was "gold in them thar hills"—that music with a western twang was a good money-maker—the whole field of country music was viewed in a new way. Before the thirties, country-and-western music had been regional in its promotion. That was about to end.

With the Ziegfeld *Follies* in 1934 came a song that was destined for a place in country music history. "Wagon Wheels," written by Billy Hill together with Peter De Rose, made its appearance in New York and won over New Yorkers as well as the "home-folk" in other areas of the country.

De Rose, the composer, went on to other successes, among them "Deep Purple." Boston-born Billy Hill, the "Wagon Wheels" lyricist, spent the remainder of his life writing cowboy songs, inspired by his 13 years in the West—in Death Valley mines, as a cowpuncher, and as a hash-house dishwasher.

Although "Wagon Wheels" was written decades after the last covered wagon had actually crossed the United States, the simplicity of the song's music and the heartfelt honesty of its lyrics seemed to recapture the spirit of the Old West. At the same time, it rekindled Americans' interest in their pioneer heritage. The combination was a winner, not only for "Wagon Wheels" but for the other country-flavored music Billy Hill produced over the years.

WAGON WHEELS

Lyric by
BILLY HILL

Music by
PETER DE ROSE

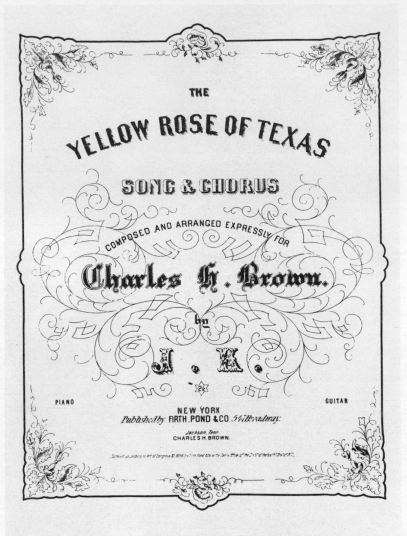

Most people who hear "The Yellow Rose Of Texas" think immediately of Mitch Miller and his sing-along group. In the mid-50s, it was Miller who popularized the song for a new, younger generation of music lovers. But anyone whose memory can stretch back 20 years before that time might remember "The Yellow Rose Of Texas" as one of President Franklin D. Roosevelt's favorites.

No one, though, can be expected to remember "The Yellow Rose Of Texas" when it was popular the first time. The song originally appeared in 1858 with only the initials "J. K." printed as the author. "J. K." was never identified, but his song became a standard with the minstrel shows of the time.

During the Civil War, "The Yellow Rose Of Texas" had the unique distinction of being a marching song for both the North and the South. It's perfectly understandable that the South would use the song, since Texas was part of the Confederacy. (The song also has been credited as being a Negro song.) Why the North used "The Yellow Rose Of Texas" as its marching song may have no other explanation than that it was a catchy, spirited tune. At any rate, the song seemed to enjoy complete neutrality during the Civil War. After the war, its lyrics became the official song of the Texas Rangers.

From show business to war duty and back to everyday popularity, "The Yellow Rose Of Texas" seems to be a perennial that's capable of surviving anything to which a music-loving public subjects it.

THE YELLOW ROSE OF TEXAS

Arranged by Frank Metis

Traditional

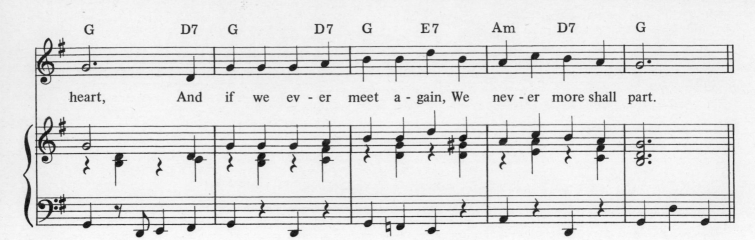

G · D7 · G · D7 · G · E7 · Am · D7 · G

heart, And if we ev - er meet a - gain, We nev - er more shall part.

Chorus: G7 · C · G · D7 · G · C · G

She's the sweet - est rose of col - or a fel - low ev - er knew, Her

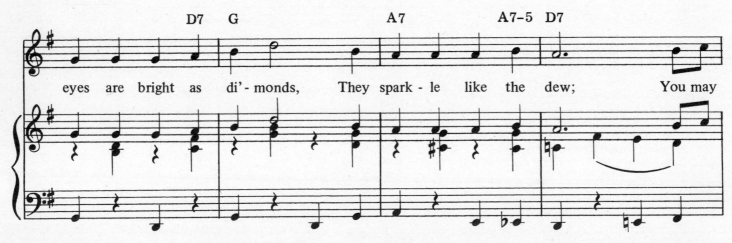

D7 · G · A7 · A7–5 · D7

eyes are bright as di'- monds, They spark - le like the dew; You may

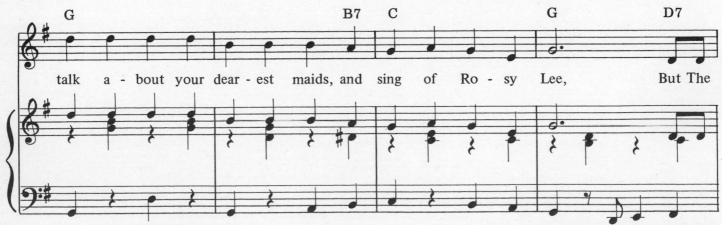

G · B7 · C · G · D7

talk a - bout your dear - est maids, and sing of Ro - sy Lee, But The

2. Where the Rio Grande is flowing,
Where stars are shining bright,
We walked along the river
On a quiet summer night;
She said, "If you remember,
We parted long ago;
You promised to come back again
And never leave me so."
(Chorus)

3. Oh, I'm going back to find her,
My heart is full of woe,
We'll sing the songs together
We sang so long ago;
I'll pick the banjo gaily,
And sing the songs of yore,
The Yellow Rose Of Texas,
She'll be mine forever more.
(Chorus)

'Way Down Yonder in New Orleans

There are few cities in the United States whose history is more intricately woven into the threads of American music than New Orleans. It's acknowledged as the birthplace of jazz and it has served as the inspiration for many popular songs, one of the best being "'Way Down Yonder In New Orleans."

The black songwriting team of Henry Creamer and Turner Layton first put their thoughts about New Orleans into music in 1922 and created a bit of musical Americana that has stood up well as a standard ever since.

"'Way Down Yonder In New Orleans" had its roots in ragtime, the pre-World War I jazz that featured an elaborately syncopated melody played against a regularly accented accompaniment. But by the twenties, pure ragtime had fallen from favor—possibly at the insistence of conservatory musicians and of Calvanist preachers who considered ragtime "artistically and morally depressing." How anyone can be depressed with the bounce and verve of ragtime is hard to imagine. At any rate, the music was put down—but only officially. Ragtime's influence survived and is felt today.

In the same way, "'Way Down Yonder In New Orleans" has survived. When first introduced, it was performed by its composers, Creamer and Layton. Then, it moved to Hollywood, showing up in the 1939 film, *The Story Of Vernon And Irene Castle.* Here, it was sung by a chorus and danced by Fred Astaire and Ginger Rogers. It hit the screen a second time in the Betty Hutton musical, *Somebody Loves Me.* And final proof of this song's endurance is that it was a best-selling hit again in 1960—this time, not by a ragtime artist, but by a country rock star. From rag to rock, "'Way Down Yonder In New Orleans" is an all-time favorite.

'WAY DOWN YONDER IN NEW ORLEANS

By HENRY CREAMER
and J. TURNER LAYTON

Verse:

Guess! Where do you think I'm go - in' when the winds start blow - in' strong?
Guess! What do you think I'm think - in' when you think I'm think - in' wrong?

Guess! Where do you think I'm go - in' when the
Guess! What do you think I'm think - in' when I'm

Dm   A7   Dm   A7   F

nights start grow-in' long?_____ I ain't go-in'East, I
think-in' all night long?_____ I ain't think-in' this, I

Bb   F   G7   G7-5   C7

ain't go-in'West, I ain't go-in' o-ver the cuck-oo's nest,__ I'm
ain't think-in' that, I can-not be think-in' a-bout your hat,__ My

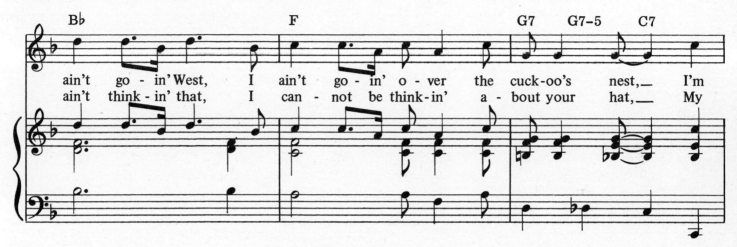

F   Bb   D7 D7-5 G7   C7

bound for the town that I love best__ Where life is one sweet song:
heart does not start to pit-a-pat__ Un-less I hear this song:

Chorus: C7 Gm7 C7   Gm7 Eb C7   F   Fmaj7

Way Down Yon-der In New Or-leans,__   In the land__ of dream-y scenes,__

mf

Other Country Classics

HELLO WALLS

Hello, Walls, how'd things go for you today?
Don't you miss her since she up and walked away?
And I'll bet you dread to spend another lonely night with me,
But, lonely walls, I'll keep you company.
Hello, window, well, I see that you're still here.
Aren't you lonely since our darlin' disappeared?
Well, look here, is that a tear drop in the corner of your pane?
Now, don't you try to tell me that it's rain.
She went away and left us all alone the way she planned.
Guess we'll have to learn to get along without her if we can.
Hello, ceiling, I'm gonna stare at you awhile,
You know I can't sleep, so won't you bear with me awhile?
We must all pull together or else I'll lose my mind,
'Cause I've got a feelin' she'll be gone a long, long time.

Words and Music by Willie Nelson

© Copyright 1961 by Tree Publishing Co., Inc.

THE LAST ROUND-UP

Chorus 1
I'm headin' for The Last Round-Up,
Gonna saddle old Paint for the last time and ride,
So long, old pal, it's time your tears were dried,
I'm headin' for The Last Round-Up.
Git along, little dogie, git along, git along, git along, little dogie,
git along,
Git along, little dogie, git along, git along, git along, little dogie,
git along.
I'm headin' for The Last Round-Up
To the far away ranch of the Boss in the Sky,
Where the strays are counted and branded, there go I,
I'm headin' for The Last Round-Up.

Chorus 2
I'm headin' for The Last Round-Up,
There'll be Buffalo Bill with his long snow white hair,
There'll be old Kit Carson and Custer waitin' there,
A-ridin' in The Last Round-Up.
Git along, little dogie, git along, git along, git along, little dogie,
git along.
Git along, little dogie, git along, git along, git along, little dogie,
git along.
I'm headin' for The Last Round-Up,
Gonna saddle old Paint for the last time and ride,
So long, old pal, it's time your tears were dried,
I'm headin' for The Last Round-Up.

Words and Music by Billy Hill

© Copyright 1933 by Shapiro, Bernstein & Co. Copyright renewed.

MAKE THE WORLD GO AWAY

Verse 1
Do you remember when you loved me
Before the world took me astray?
If you do, then forgive me,
And Make The World Go Away.

Chorus
Make the World Go Away,
And get it off my shoulders,
Say the things you used to say,
And Make The World Go Away.

Verse 2
I'm sorry if I hurt you,
I'll make it up day by day.
Just say you love me like you used to,
And Make The World Go Away.

Words and Music by Hank Cochran

© Copyright 1963 by Tree Publishing Co., Inc.

A WORRIED MAN

Chorus
It takes A Worried Man to sing a worried song.
It takes A Worried Man to sing a worried song.
It takes A Worried Man to sing a worried song.
I'm worried now, but I won't be long.

Verse 1
Got myself a Cadillac, thirty dollars down;
Got myself a brand new house five miles out of town;
Got myself a gal named Sue, treats me really fine;
Yes, she's my baby and I love her all the time.

Verse 2
I've been away on a bus'ness trip, trav'lin' all around;
I've got a gal and her name is Sue, prettiest gal in town;
She sets my mind to worryin' ev'ry time I'm gone;
I'll be home tonight, so I won't be worried long.

Verse 3
Well, Bobby's in the living room, holding hands with Sue;
Nickie's at the big front door, 'bout to come on thru;
Well, I'm here in the closet, oh Lord, what shall I do?
We're worried now, but we won't be worried long.

Words and Music by Dave Guard and Tom Glazer

© Copyright 1959 by Harvard Music, Inc.

Sole selling agent: Ivan Mogull Music Corporation.

HEARTBREAK HOTEL

Since my baby left me, found a new place to dwell.
Down at the end of Lonely Street at Heartbreak Hotel.
I get so lonely, baby, I get so lonely,
I get so lonely I could die.

Although it's always crowded, still can find some room,
Where those broken-hearted lovers cry away their gloom.
Oh! I get so lonely, I get so lonely,
Get so lonely I could die.

Bellhop's tears keep flowing, desk clerk's dressed in black,
They been so long on Lonely Street, they ain't never gonna' come back.
Oh! I get so lonely, I get so lonely,
Get so lonely I could die.

If your baby leaves you and you have a tale to tell,
Just take a walk down Lonely Street to Heartbreak Hotel.
I get so lonely, baby, I get so lonely,
I get so lonely I could die.

Words and Music by Mae Boren Axton, Tommy Durden, and Elvis Presley

© Copyright 1956 by Tree Publishing Co., Inc.

HEARTACHES BY THE NUMBER

Verse 1
Heartache Number One was when you left me,
I never knew that I could hurt this way.
And Heartache Number Two was when you came back again,
You came back and never meant to stay.

Chorus
Now I've got Heartaches By The Number, troubles by the score.
Ev'ry day you love me less, each day I love you more.
Yes, I've got Heartaches By The Number, a love that I can't win,
But the day that I stop counting, that's the day my world will end.

Verse 2
Heartache Number three was when you called me,
And said that you were coming back to stay.
With hopeful heart I waited for your knock on the door,
I waited but you must have lost your way.

Words and Music by Harlan Howard

© Copyright 1959 by Tree Publishing Co., Inc.

YOU CAN HAVE HIM

Chorus
You Can Have Him, I don't want him,
He didn't love me anyway.
He only wanted someone to play with,
But all I wanted was love to stay.

Verse 1
Well, if you get the wrong fella,
There's only one thing that you can do:
Just dig a hole and jump right in it,
And pull the ground right over you.

Verse 2
The boy I love, he up and left me,
He ran away with my best friend.
Comes home at night just for an hour,
When daylight comes, he's gone again.

Verse 3
Life without love is mighty empty,
Confession is good for the soul.
I'd rather have love that I can cling to,
Than have the world and all its gold.

Words and Music by Bill Cook

© Copyright 1960 by Harvard Music Inc. and Big Billy Music Co.

Sole selling agent: Ivan Mogull Music Corporation.

DON'T DO IT, DARLING

Verse
There was once a time I couldn't get you off my mind,
Thru cloudy days and lonely nights I'd sit alone and pine.
You promised you'd be true,
And we would never part.
I believed in you.
So you could break my heart.

Chorus
If you worry over me
Like I worried over you,
Don't Do It, Darling!
Don't Do It, Darling!
If you think I'm missing you,
And I'm missing kissing you,
Don't Do It, Darling!
Don't Do It, Darling!
I gave you all the love I had,
And trusted it with you;
You took my heart and played with it,
And then you proved untrue.
Now that you are all alone
And you fell the urge to phone.
Don't Do It Darling!
Don't Do It Darling!

Words and Music by Zeke Manners

© Copyright 1942 by Shapiro, Bernstein & Co. Copyright renewed.

Songs of Battle

A country's music mirrors her feelings—especially during times of war. It's the nation's songwriters who speak for the whole nation, who are able to put down in words and music what the rest of the country feels but can't express.

Over the years, America's wartime music has played many roles—everything from leading our soldiers into battle to easing the loneliness of the mothers and sweethearts left at home. Almost every war or military conflict has produced some lasting music.

Up until the Civil War, our soldiers seem to have made do with parodies of English battle songs, but with the War Between the States, each side produced a song that became its rallying cry. It should be mentioned, however, that although each side had its song, the Confederacy's "Dixie's Land" was written by a Northerner and "Battle Hymn Of The Republic" was composed by a Southerner. It took a little transposition before each army had its own song and had it revised just the way they wanted it.

There was one memorable Civil War song, however, that expressed the feelings of both sides. "When Johnny Comes Marching Home Again" was introduced in 1863 and has seen service in every military involvement since that time.

Now, more than one hundred years since the Civil War guns were muted, there is no partisanship where these great songs are concerned. These compositions are American!

The music of World Wars I and II is also unquestionably American in its expression of wartime attitudes. During World War I, songwriters lyricized some of the strongest sentiments ever put to music. But with World War II, battle songs shifted emphasis and became subtle messages of encouragement, praise, or hope for peace.

Korea produced no memorable songs, but Vietnam did. A song by Sgt. Barry Sadler, "The Ballad Of The Green Berets," is the most recent addition to a long list of American songs of battle, yet it's a song that will live on to musically represent another battlefront.

From the time that the walls of Jericho were leveled by trumpets to the writing of the song "The Ballad Of The Green Berets," war has produced a music all its own.

Battle Hymn of the Republic

Julia Ward Howe wrote the words to "Battle Hymn Of The Republic," which later became the Union's soldiering song, when she was visiting Washington with her husband and a few friends in the fall of 1861. One day, the group visited an army camp, and it was there where she first heard the "Glory, Glory, Hallelujah" melody to which she wrote lyrics.

The tune, written by William Steffe, a Richmond, Virginia composer of Sunday-school songs, had been around for about ten years. With Steffe's words, "Say, brothers will you meet us?" the melody soon was widely known and other lyricists were concocting topical verses for it. Of these, the most famous version was "John Brown's Body," which was inspired not by the fellow who raided Harper's Ferry but by a Scotsman who was a member of an independent battalion of the Massachusetts Infantry. He and a few of his fellow soldiers had formed a glee club, and they'd often sing as they worked away with their picks and shovels. After the Harper's Ferry raid, people who heard the glee club's song thought the song referred to the abolitionist. Still other lyricists added verses about the raid itself. After a military band of the day added "John Brown's Body" to its repertoire, everybody was singing it.

At any rate, when Mrs. Howe heard the song, she thought the lyrics were "inadequate for a lasting hymn," but the tune she found catchy, so one of her companions suggested that she try composing something more suitable. That night before dawn she woke up suddenly. The first lines had come to her while she was asleep. She was soon scribbling away with a stub of pencil. The Atlantic Monthly published her poem in February, 1862.

BATTLE HYMN OF THE REPUBLIC

Words and Music by
W. STEFFE and
JULIA WARD HOWE

Arranged by Frank Metis

Moderately

1. Mine eyes have seen the glo - ry of the com - ing of the Lord, He is
2. (I have) seen Him in the watch - fires of a hun - dred cir - cling camps, They have

tram - pling out the vin - tage where the grapes of wrath are stored. He has
build - ed Him an al - tar in the eve - ning dews and damps. I can

loosed the fate - ful light - ning of His ter - ri - ble swift sword, His
read His right - eous sen - tence by the dim and flar - ing lamps, His

Chorus:

truth is march-ing on.
day is march-ing on.

Glo - ry, Glo - ry Hal - le - lu - jah!

Glo - ry, Glo - ry Hal - le - lu - jah!

Glo - ry, Glo - ry Hal - le -

lu - jah! His truth is march-ing on!

2. I have on!

3. He has sounded forth the trumpet that
      shall never call retreat;
   He is sifting out the hearts of men before
      His judgement seat.
   Oh, be swift, my soul, to answer Him!
      Be jubilant my feet!
   Our God is marching on!
   (Chorus)

THE MARINES' HYMN

As approved and authorized by
UNITED STATES MARINE CORPS

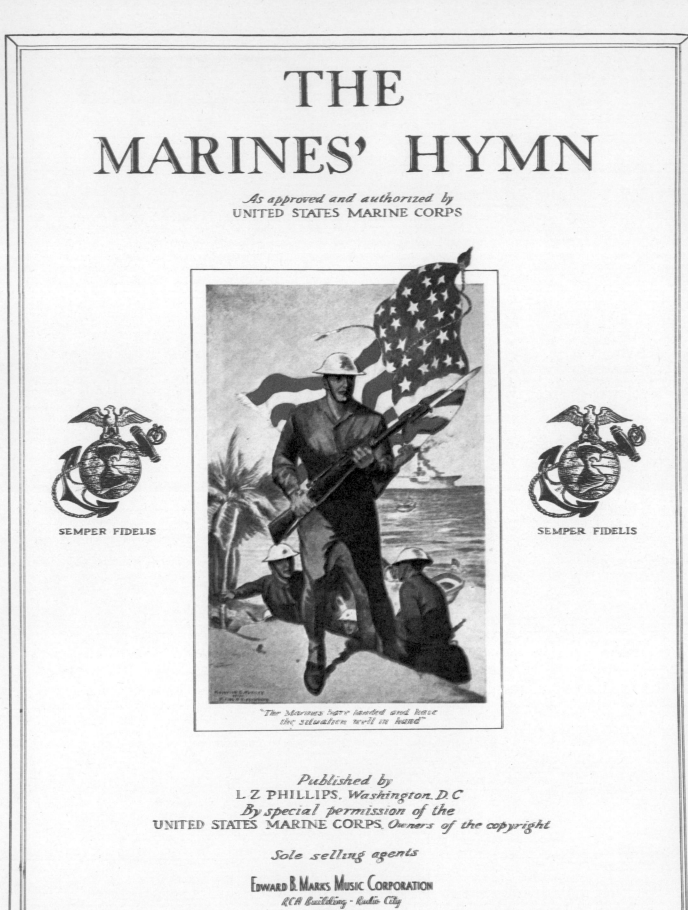

SEMPER FIDELIS

SEMPER FIDELIS

"The Marines have landed and have the situation well in hand"

Published by
L Z PHILLIPS, *Washington, D.C*
By special permission of the
UNITED STATES MARINE CORPS, *Owners of the copyright*

Sole selling agents

EDWARD B. MARKS MUSIC CORPORATION
RCA Building - Radio City
NEW YORK

The Marines' Hymn

When the United States Marine Corps was established by an Act of Congress dated June 25, 1776, it probably was "Yankee Doodle" that spurred the men to battle. Later-day Leathernecks, however, have had their own "Marines' Hymn," first published in 1918. Its melody comes from French composer Jacques Offenbach's "Couplets des Deux Hommes d'Armes," a march first sung in an 1859 opera.

The writer of the hymn's lyrics is unknown, and as might be expected, speculation has arisen as to whom he might have been and in what campaigns he might have served. Advocates of one theory say that he was a member of the Marine Corps during World War I, since the publication date coincides with that time. Others insist, basing their opinion on the lyrics "From the Halls of Montezuma," that he was a member of a battalion of 40 men who, during the United States war with Mexico, landed at Vera Cruz, Mexico, in March, 1847, took Mexico City late that summer, and thus put an end to the troublesome war.

The continuation of the same line of lyrics, "to the shores of Tripoli," however, leads others to believe that he was one of a detachment of 16 Marines and 40 Greek mercenaries, who, mounted on a fleet of camels and led by a former Army officer, William Eaton, marched 500 miles across the desert from Alexandria, Egypt, to Tripoli, on the Libyan coast to recapture a U.S. Navy warship being held captive by pirates. (The ship had run aground on a mission to rescue American merchant seamen who were being held for ransom.)

Although it's doubtful we'll ever know who it was, this person's respect for the United States Marine Corps resulted in a tribute to some of America's bravest men.

THE MARINES' HYMN

Arranged by Rosamond Johnson

Words and Music by
L.Z. PHILLIPS

March

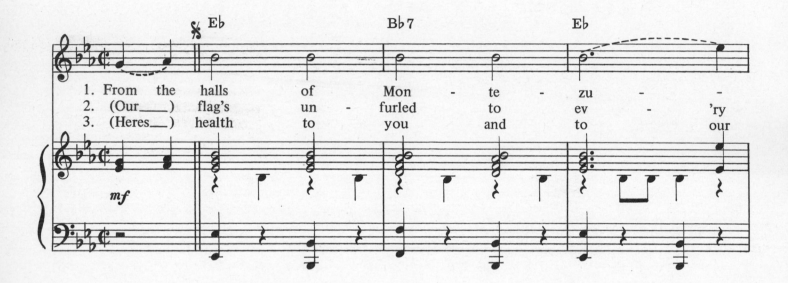

1. From the halls of Mon - te - zu - - ma, To the shores of Tri - po - li. ____
2. (Our___) flag's un - furled to ev - 'ry breeze, From_ dawn to set - ting sun, ____
3. (Heres___) health to you and to our Corps, Which_ we are proud to serve; ____

The original "Yankee Doodle" marched along with the troops during the American Revolution. Though the exact origin of the Colonists' "Yankee Doodle" is not known, it's generally considered to be an English import.

The origin of "Yankee Doodle Dandy," however, is perfectly clear and possibly within the recall of some of America's senior citizens. It was in 1904 when Broadway's all-time great patriot, George M. Cohan, introduced on stage a spirited song called "Yankee Doodle Boy." He penned it for his first full-length musical, *Little Johnny Jones*, and it was Cohan himself who performed the song. Some while later, the song's title was changed to "Yankee Doodle Dandy," and in 1942 James Cagney won an Academy Award for his portrayal of Cohan in a musical biography of the same name.

Only Cohan could have created "Yankee Doodle Dandy." He was truly a "real, live nephew of my Uncle Sam," and though poetic license caused him to delay his birthday from July 3rd to the Fourth of July, his patriotism was irrefutable.

Since its introduction, "Yankee Doodle Dandy" has been sung, hummed, and whistled by soldiers in two World Wars and several military conflicts. Whenever the patriotism of Americans is displayed, chances are "Yankee Doodle Dandy" will be part of the musical fireworks.

(I'M A) YANKEE DOODLE DANDY

Words and Music by
GEORGE M. COHAN

March

Verse:

I'm the kid that's all the can-dy, I'm a Yan-kee Doo-dle Dan-dy,
Fa-ther's name was Hez-i-ki-ah, Moth-er's name was Ann Ma-ri-a,

I'm glad I am; So's 'Un-cle Sam.
Yanks, through and through! Red, White and Blue.

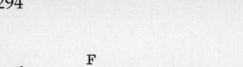

I'm a real live Yan-kee Doo-dle, Made my name and fame and boo-dle,
Fa-ther was so Yan-kee heart-ed, When the Span-ish war was start-ed,

Just like Mis-ter Doo-dle did by rid-ing on a po-ny. I
He slipped on his un-i-form and hopped up-on a po-ny. My

love to lis-ten to the Dix-ie strain, I long to see the girl I
moth-er's moth-er was a Yan-kee, true, My fa-ther's fa-ther was a

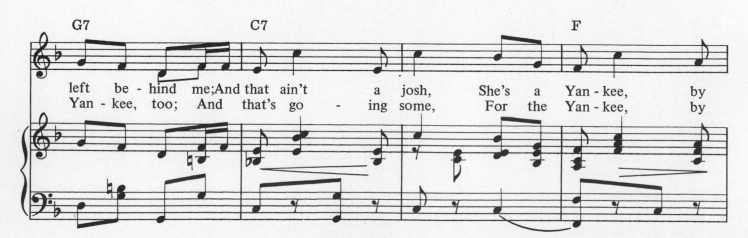

left be-hind me;And that ain't a josh, She's a Yan-kee, by
Yan-kee, too; And that's go-ing some, For the Yan-kee, by

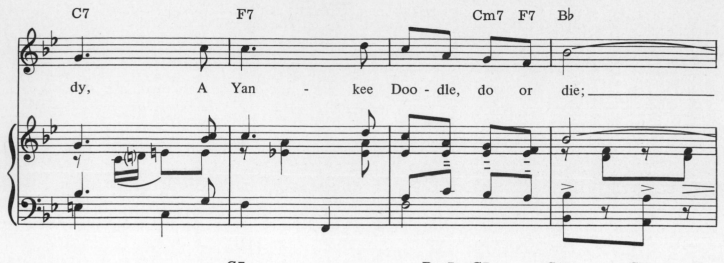

dy, A Yan - kee Doo - dle, do or die; _____

_____ A real live neph - ew of my Un - cle

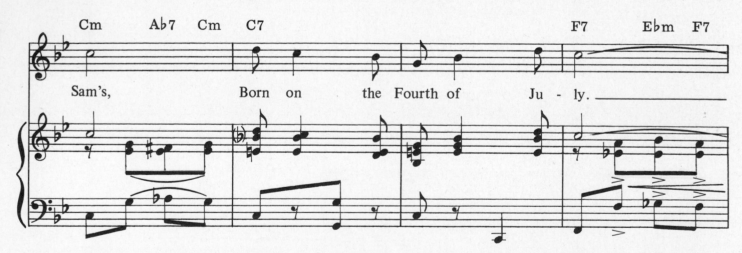

Sam's, Born on the Fourth of Ju - ly. _____

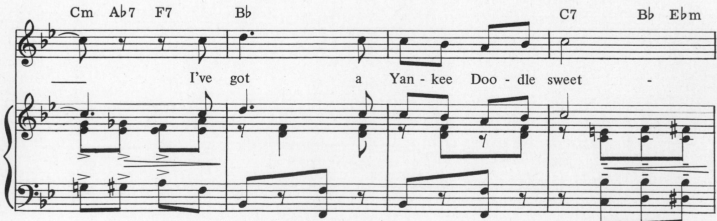

_____ I've got a Yan - kee Doo - dle sweet -

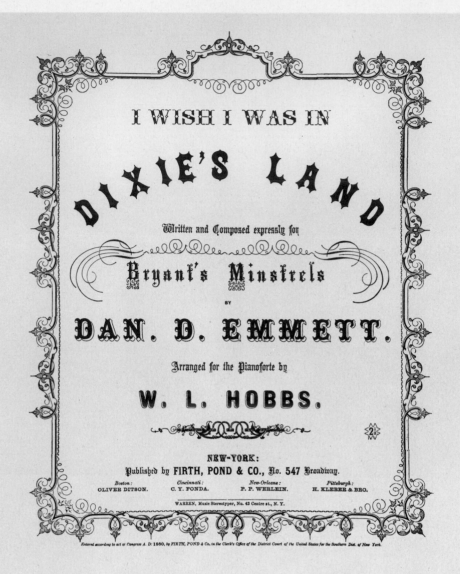

I WISH I WAS IN

DIXIE'S LAND

Written and Composed expressly for

Bryant's Minstrels

BY

DAN. D. EMMETT.

Arranged for the Pianoforte by

W. L. HOBBS.

NEW-YORK:
Published by FIRTH, POND & CO., No. 547 Broadway.

Boston: OLIVER DITSON. *Cincinnati:* C. Y. FONDA. *New-Orleans:* P. P. WERLEIN. *Pittsburgh:* H. KLEBER & BRO.

WARREN, Music Stereotyper, No. 43 Centre st., N. Y.

Entered according to act of Congress A. D. 1860, by FIRTH, POND & Co., in the Clerk's Office of the District Court of the United States for the Southern Dist. of New York.

Although "Dixie Land" stirred Confederate soldiers during the Civil War, it was written by a Northerner, with no thoughts of it being a war song. Its original title was "Dixie's Land," and Daniel Decatur Emmett wrote this song as a minstrel show "walkaround," the closing number in which the entire company paraded around the stage. The year was 1859 and Emmett was spending a cold, rainy Sunday afternoon in his New York boarding house. His thoughts drifted to warmer climates and he commented to his wife, "I wish I was in Dixie." In Emmett's words, "Suddenly I jumped up and sat down at the table to work. In less than an hour I had the first verse and chorus. After that it was easy."

The first southern performance of the tune took place in Charleston, South Carolina, in 1860. Musical historians, however, date the real beginning of "Dixie Land's" southern popularity to 1861 and a performance given in New Orleans.

The song then underwent several lyric changes to suit whatever needs it was fulfilling. "Dixie Land" has served as a battle song, a campaign song against the election of President Lincoln in 1860, and the victory song of nearly every southern college. The black dialect of the original song has been changed as has the title, but Dan Emmett's "Dixie's Land" has survived it all.

DIXIE LAND

Words and Music by
DAN D. EMMETT

Arranged by Frank Metis

Lively

Verse:

C   F

1. I___ wish I was_ in de land ob cot - ton, Old times dar am
2. (Dar's_) buck-wheat cakes_ an'_ In - gen bat - ter, Makes you fat or a

mf

C

not for - got - ten, Look a - way!   Look a - way!   Look a -
lit - tle fat - ter, Look a - way!   Look a - way!   Look a -

G   C

way!   Dix - ie Land!   In ___ Dix - ie Land_ whar_
way!   Dix - ie Land!   Den hoe it down_ an___

300

I was born in, Ear - ly on one frost - y morn - in', Look a -
scratch your grab - ble, To Dix - ie Land I'm bound to trab - ble, Look a -

way! Look a - way! Look a - way! Dix - ie Land!
way! Look a - way! Look a - way! Dix - ie Land!

Chorus:

Den I wish I was in Dix - ie, Hoo - ray! Hoo -

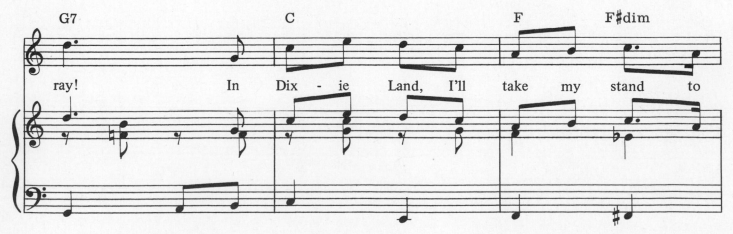

ray! In Dix - ie Land, I'll take my stand to

lib and die in Dix - ie. A - way, A - way, A -

way down south in Dix - ie, A - way, A - way, A -

way down south in Dix - ie.

2. Dar's_ A - way down south in Dix - ie.

Other Songs of Battle

TRAMP, TRAMP, TRAMP!

Verse 1
On the battle front we stand, 'neath the flag that made us free,
Ever ready at the word to do and dare;
Tho' we're twice a million strong, still they're coming from the sea,
We can hear the tread like thunder in the air.

Chorus
Tramp, Tramp, Tramp! The boys are marching!
Cheer, brave comrades, they will come;
Ev'ry heart is in the fight for the cause of Truth and Right
And the freedom of our own beloved land!

Verse 2
They are coming from the West, you can hear the mighty roar,
As they tramp the earth and sing a battle song;
There are millions in the fight, and as many millions more
Only wait the nation's call to come along.

Verse 3
There's a God in glory still and his word is on the sky,
Blazing letters for the dastard foe to read:
Ye are traitors to the truth and as traitors ye shall die,
Tho' a world be made to suffer and to bleed!

Words by David Stevens   Music by George F. Root

THEY'RE EITHER TOO YOUNG OR TOO OLD

Verse
You marched away and left this town as empty as can be,
I can't sit under the apple tree with anyone else but me.
For there is no secret lover that the draft board didn't discover:

Chorus
They're Either Too Young Or Too Old,
They're either too gray or too grassy green,
The pickin's are poor and the crop is lean,
What's good is in the army, what's left will never harm me.
They're either too old or too young,
So darling, you'll never get stung.
Tomorrow I'll go hiking with that Eagle Scout unless
I get a call from grandpa for a snappy game of chess.
I'm finding it easy to stay good as gold.
They're Either Too Young Or Too Old.
I'll never, never fail ya, while you are in Australia,
Or out in the Aleutians, or off among the Rooshians
And flying over Egypt, your heart will never be gypped,
And when you get to India, I'll still be what I've been to ya.
I've looked the field over and lo, and behold,
They're Either Too Young Or Too Old!

Words by Frank Loesser   Music by Arthur Schwartz
© Copyright 1943 by M. Witmark & Sons. Copyright renewed.

THE BALLAD OF THE GREEN BERETS

Verse 1
Fighting soldiers from the sky,
Fearless men who jump and die.
Men who mean just what they say,
The brave men of the Green Beret.

Chorus 1
Silver wings upon their chests,
These are men, America's best.
One hundred men we'll test today,
But only three win the Green Beret.

Verse 2
Trained to live off nature's land,
Trained to combat, hand to hand.
Men who fight by night and day,
Courage take from the Green Beret.

Chorus 2
Silver wings upon their chests,
These are men, America's best.
One hundred men we'll test today,
But only three win the Green Beret.

Verse 3
Back at home a young wife waits,
Her Green Beret has met his fate.
He has died for those oppressed,
Leaving her this last request:

Chorus 3
Put silver wings on my son's chest,
Make him one of America's best.
He'll be a man they'll test one day,
Have him win the Green Beret.

Words and Music by Barry Sadler and Robin Moore
© Copyright 1963, 1964 and 1966 by Music Music Music Inc.

WHEN JOHNNY COMES MARCHING HOME

When Johnny comes marching home again, Hurrah! Hurrah!
We'll give him a hearty welcome then, Hurrah! Hurrah!
The men will cheer, the boys will shout, the ladies they will all turn out,
And we'll all feel gay When Johnny Comes Marching Home!

The old church bell will peal with joy, Hurrah! Hurrah!
To welcome home our darling boy, Hurrah! Hurrah!
The village lads and lassies gay, with roses they will strew the way,
And we'll all feel gay When Johnny Comes Marching Home!

Get ready for the jubilee, Hurrah! Hurrah!
We'll give the heros three times three, Hurrah! Hurrah!
The laurel wreath is ready now to place upon his loyal brow,
And we'll all feel gay When Johnny Comes Marching Home!

WE DID IT BEFORE

(We'll Do It Again)

Verse
December seventh, nineteen hundred and forty one,
Our land of freedom was defied;
December eighth, nineteen hundred and forty one
Uncle Sam replied:

Chorus
We Did It Before and we can do it again and we will do it again,
We've got a heck of a job to do, but you can bet that we'll see it thru.
We Did It Before and we can do it again and we will do it again,
We're one for all and we're all for one,
They'll get a lickin' before we're done.
Millions of voices are ringing,
Singing as we march along…
We Did It Before and we can do it again and we will do it again
We'll knock them over and then we'll get the guy in back of them
We Did It Before, we'll do it again.

Words and Music by Cliff Friend and Charlie Tobias
© Copyright 1941 by M. Witmarck & Sons. Copyright renewed.

ON, BRAVE OLD ARMY TEAM

Verse
The Army team's the pride and dream of every heart in gray,
The Army line you'll ever find a terror in the fray.
And when the team is fighting
For the Black and Gray and Gold,
We're always near with song and cheer
And this is the tale we're told:
The Army team Rah! Rah! Rah! Boom!

Chorus
On, Brave Old Army Team!
On to the fray,
Fight on to Victory
For that's the fearless Army way.

Words and Music by Philip Egner
© Copyright 1911 by Shapiro, Bernstein & Co. Copyright renewed 1938.

THERE'S SOMETHING ABOUT A SOLDIER

Verse
When they march down the street,
People stand on your feet,
They love to see a soldier.
Tho' they jump on your chest,
You fall in with the rest,
You want to see a soldier.
You will run half a mile,
But it's well worth your while,
Because somebody has told ya,
That in the Palace Yard
You'll see the changing of the guard,
Oh! How you run to see a soldier.

Chorus
Because There's Something About A Soldier,
Something about a soldier,
Something about a soldier, that is fine, fine, fine.
He may be a great big Gen'ral,
Maybe a Sergeant Major,
Maybe a simple private on the line, line, line,
But there's something about his bearing,
Something in what he's wearing,
Something about his buttons all a-shine, shine, shine.
Oh! A military chest seems to suit the ladies best,
There's Something About A Soldier that is fine, fine, fine!

Words and Music by Noel Gay
© Copyright 1933 by Lawrence Wright Music Co. Ltd. Copyright renewed 1961.
Exclusive Publisher in the U.S.A. and Canada, Mills Music, Inc.

HE WEARS A PAIR OF SILVER WINGS

Verse
It's just a simple love affair,
Two people met, they learned to care,
And found themselves in heaven.
To you, maybe the story's nothing new,
To me, it's all my wildest dreams come true:

Chorus
Altho' some people say he's just a crazy guy,
To me he means a million other things,
For he's the one who taught this happy heart of mine to fly,
He Wears A Pair Of Silver Wings.
And tho' it's pretty tough, the job he does above,
I wouldn't have him change it for a king's,
An ordinary fellow in the uniform I love,
He Wears A Pair Of Silver Wings.
I'm so full of pride when we go walking
Ev'ry time he's home on leave,
He with those wings on his tunic,
Me with my heart on my sleeve.
But when I'm left alone and we are far apart,
I sometimes wonder what tomorrow brings,
For I adore that crazy guy who taught my happy heart
To wear a pair of silver wings.

Words by Eric Maschwitz   Music by Michael Carr
© Copyright 1941 by Peter Maurice Music Co. Copyright renewed.
Sole selling agent: Shapiro, Bernstein & Co., Inc.

Index

Credits

Sheet music covers: Courtesy of the publisher. Covers on pages 14, 82, 86, 90, 96, 122, 186, and 272 obtained from the collection of Lloyd Keepers.

Photographs and illustrations: Page 11—The Granger Collection. 15—Culver Pictures. 35—Edward Steichen. 40—Camera 5 (Ken Regan). 53—The Bettmann Archive. 65—Magnum (Ernst Haas). 70—Brown Brothers. 102 —Antiques/Plus, Zellwood, Florida. 123—Brown Brothers. 133— The Granger Collection. 137— By permission from "old" Life. 142—Hy Fujita. 212—Painting by John Ham and used by permission of Standard Publishing, Cincinnati, Ohio. 216—Courtesy The Hermitage Art Company, Inc., Chicago, Illinois. 231—Courtesy Al "Jazzbeaux" Collins. 287— Courtesy U.S. Marine Corps, Department of Defense photo.

maj - es - ties A - bove the fruit-ed

shed His grace on thee, And crown thy g